Let's Build:

Strong Foundations in Language, Math, and Social Skills

by Pamela C. Phelps

DEDICATION

This book is dedicated to all children who have loved playing with the Creative Pre-School blocks and to the teachers who have made the experience unique, first Ms. Martha Pleas, and later Ms. Susan Brooks and Mr. Chuck Alexander.

Let's
BUILD

Strong
Foundations
in Language,
Math, and
Social Skills

Pamela C. Phelps

Gryphon
House, Inc.
Lewisville, NC

©2012 Pamela C. Phelps

Published by Gryphon House, Inc.
PO Box 10, Lewisville, NC 27023
800.638.0928; 877.638.7576 (fax)

Visit us on the web at www.gryphonhouse.com.

Cover photograph courtesy of Kaplan Early Learning Co., Lewisville, NC.

Interior photographs: © iStock photo LP 2011. All rights reserved. IStockphoto® and iStock® re trademarks of iStockphoto LP. www.istockphoto.com.

Library of Congress Cataloging-in-Publication Data

Phelps, Pamela C.

Let's build : strong foundations in language, math, and social skills / by Pamela C. Phelps.

  p. cm.

Includes bibliographical references and index.

ISBN 978-0-87659-396-7

1. Early childhood education--Activity programs. 2. Language arts (Early childhood)--Activity programs. 3. Social skills--Study and teaching (Early childhood)--Activity programs. 4. Blocks (Toys) in mathematics education. 5. Blocks (Toys) I. Title.

LB1139.35.A37P44 2012

372.21--dc23

2012004313

Bulk Purchase
Gryphon House books are available for special premiums and sales promotions as well as for fund-raising use. Special editions or book excerpts also can be created to specifications. For details, contact the Director of Marketing at Gryphon House.

Disclaimer
Gryphon House, Inc. cannot be held responsible for damage, mishap, or injury incurred during the use of or because of activities in this book. Appropriate and reasonable caution and adult supervision of children involved in activities, corresponding to the age and capability of each child involved, is recommended at all times. Do not leave children unattended at any time. Observe safety and caution at all times.

Table of Contents

LET'S BUILD: Strong Foundations in Language, Math, and Social Skills

LET'S BUILD: Strong Foundations in Language, Math, and Social Skills

Preface

The block area in any and every childhood program can be a welcoming space for both boys and girls. Blocks are marvelous play materials that offer many learning opportunities. This book is for teachers who know and understand the learning potential of blocks and for teachers who know that books are valuable classroom materials but need help understanding why blocks are important and how to use blocks effectively (and playfully) in the classroom.

One person who understood and valued construction play with blocks was Carolyn Pratt, who designed the basic wooden unit blocks used in early childhood classrooms.

As Ms. Martha Pleas at the Creative Pre-School (1973–1998) explored the block-play possibilities with children, she would often say, "Now when you use Ms. Carolyn Pratt's blocks, you can make anything you want. Look at the pictures in your mind and make them out of her blocks."

Children who play at the Creative Pre-School in Tallahassee, Florida, have used the same set of Ms. Carolyn's blocks for more than 40 years. Some of children who attend this school today are children of the first children who went to Creative Pre-School. Today's children play with the same blocks because blocks are an almost-forever toy. The sounds of joy and accomplishment fill the classrooms as children use their imagination to make blocks become whatever they want or need in their play. Many adults, who played with these blocks as young children—both boys and girls—have used the knowledge they gained from their experiences and applied it to their careers, which include architecture and engineering.

Pam Phelps, the author of this book, first started Creative Pre-School in 1971. Before children played in the block area, she would tell them about a woman, Carolyn Pratt, who wanted children in her school to have special things to play with. Dr. Phelps told the children about how Carolyn Pratt went to the docks of New York City and collected pieces of wood so children could construct the buildings and other structures they saw around them. Blocks were a major focus of the *Beyond Centers and Circle Time Curriculum* (2002), which was perfected at Creative Pre-School, where it remains a focal point today. The block center at Creative Pre-School offers children an array of more than 4,000 different kinds of blocks to use in their unique, imaginative constructions.

When children play with blocks, they have numerous opportunities to learn, develop, and refine mathematical knowledge and social and language skills. Playing with blocks is a golden learning experience.

Introduction

In a world in which many play materials are designed for a single purpose with batteries that make them beep and sparkle with lights, nothing is left to the imagination of young children. When toys are designed to imitate the objects they represent, it limits how the toy can be used. Ideally, toys should give children open-ended opportunities to use their imaginations and creativity. Toys like blocks create numerous and varied ways to develop children's minds.

David Elkind, psychologist, well-known advocate for children, and author of *The Power of Play* (2007), stresses the importance of play and the value of experiences that offer children opportunities to experiment with water, sand, and other natural materials. Wooden blocks are the ultimate natural play material for children. Holding a block and feeling its smooth finish, smelling its natural aroma, and seeing its earthy coloring is a very different sensory experience from interacting with a brightly colored plastic toy with an explicit design. In addition, block play gives children the ability to use their imagination to build and construct what they need for their play, to make plans, to carry out their plans, to problem-solve any challenges, to navigate roles and responsibilities with their co-builders, and to learn many other skills as they plan and build their constructions.

Children naturally do many of the things that help them grow and develop. The baby who is learning to adjust to his mother leaving and returning will engage in "peekaboo" games, and the three-year-old who is learning to enjoy the sounds of words will play with rhyming sounds as she soaks in the tub of bubble water at night. When adults guide and support children who are developing a new or difficult-to-learn task or developmental milestone, true learning can take place. Perhaps this is what Jean-Jacques Rousseau, an eighteenth-century philosopher, observed in the behavior of young children that led him to believe in their innate abilities to learn and develop.

Recently, some aspects of brain research along with federal and state legislation have created an educational environment that focuses on the memorization of specific knowledge and diminishing opportunities for play. Research shows, however, that well-planned play opportunities with teacher

LET'S BUILD: Strong Foundations in Language, Math, and Social Skills

guidance and support (also called scaffolding) provide the best of both worlds—a world in which the specific information children need to know, such as number knowledge, phonemic awareness, and print awareness, can be embedded into meaningful play (Hanline, Milton, and Phelps 2009; Berk and Winsler 1995; Christie and Roskos 2006). Young children whose early experiences include reading books, conversations about what is happening, and time to explore and discover the things in their lives that interest them, may not need as much teacher guidance and support as they play.

Young children need opportunities to discover knowledge. For this to happen, the adults involved must understand both how children learn and the content and skills that they must learn. State and federal early-learning standards guide the content provided for preschool children in early care and education programs. These standards provide a shared framework for understanding and communicating expectations about young children's development. The standards written by different groups of people with varying backgrounds have consistently divided child development into the following domains of development.

- ❏ Physical Development

- ❏ Approaches to Learning

- ❏ Social and Emotional Development

- ❏ Language and Communication

- ❏ Cognitive Development and General Knowledge

Although some states have expanded the standards to six or even eight domains, the content is virtually the same. Many states, such as Rhode Island, have chosen to emphasize the importance of **_play_** as the vehicle that should drive all early-learning experiences.

> **Play appears as the first Learning Goal in each domain. The Early Learning Standards reflect Rhode Island's strong belief in the important role of play in how children learn. Through play, children enhance the learning of skills, knowledge, and dispositions that guarantees success in later schooling.**
>
> **—From the Rhode Island Early Learning Standards**

Ellen Galinsky in her book, *Mind in the Making* (2010) examines the results of research that was conducted to discover how children learn best. Her work has resulted in the following list of seven essential skills every child must develop to become successful, not just in school but in life:

Skill #1: The ability to focus and exercise self-control

Skill #2: The ability to notice and understand the needs of others

Skill #3: The ability to communicate

Skill #4: The ability to make connections (what fits together)

Skill #5: The ability to think critically

Skill #6: The ability to take on challenges

Skill #7: The ability to direct their own learning and seek knowledge

What better place to learn and practice these skills than in a well-developed, teacher-scaffolded block area?

Early childhood educators know and understand that children can discover and create their own knowledge and that this is how young children learn best.

This book is written to offer guidance to early child educators who want to create learning environments that support children's natural need to play. Through well-planned and teacher-supported experiences, children can discover and use math, science, literacy, and social knowledge. This knowledge is the foundation that will help children develop a love of learning and a trust in their own abilities (Galinksy 2010). It isn't the specific, memorized knowledge that children need to learn. Instead, they need to develop the ability to think critically, problem solve, and seek knowledge and information. In today's world, specific knowledge is available almost instantaneously, but whether this information is correct or how to use it effectively will depend upon the creative thinkers of tomorrow. Learning to think creatively, to think outside the box, begins when children have the opportunity and support to **play** during their early years (Brown and Vaughn 2009).

The History of Blocks

Children have played with sticks for centuries. Children pick up sticks lying on the ground and instantly transform the sticks into any number of objects: a candle for a mud birthday cake, a spoon to stir a pot of soup, a shovel to dig a hole, and, of course, a weapon. How children use sticks is entirely dependent on their imagination. A four-year-old might say, "A stick can be anything I want it to be," Because sticks are so important to children's play, the stick has been entered into the National Toy Hall of Fame.

When it comes to good toys, there is nothing better than something simple, something that is open-ended and limitless in its possibilities for play (Bowman 2009).

As long ago as the age in which Plato taught and struggled to create a new form of government, a new way for people to learn and take control over their lives, play was discussed as the vehicle that would develop citizens who could not only live in a society but who also would be contributing members. The following quote is a conversation between Socrates and Plato's brother Glaucon that can be found in *The Republic:*

"Well then, the study of calculation and geometry, and all the preparatory education required for dialectic must be put before them as children, and the instruction must not be given the aspect of a compulsion to learn."

"Why not?"

"Because the free man ought not to learn any study slavishly. Forced labors performed by the body don't make the body any worse, but no forced study abides in the soul."

"True," he said.

"Therefore, you best of men," I said, "don't use force in training the children in the subjects, **but rather play.** In that way, you can better discern what each is naturally directed toward."

Plato, a student of Socrates, is credited with writing many of his dialogues that provide insight into the philosopher's beliefs and teachings.

Johann Pestalozzi was a student of Jean-Jacques Rousseau, who also believed that children were born good and that they needed to be nurtured gently. The Pestalozzi Method of education became a reality in his school at Yverdon (established in 1805). He argued that children should learn through activity and by interacting with objects. He believed that children should be free to pursue their own interests and draw their own conclusions (Darling 1994, 18).

The Beginning of Block Play

Frederick Froebel transformed pieces of wood for children into specific geometric shapes more than 200 years ago. Froebel, who is known as the father of the Kindergarten, created "gifts" for children in his school to manipulate. Six of the ten "gifts" he created were wooden geometric shapes. He believed that as children interacted with the shapes, their experiences would prepare their minds for higher learning and would connect the children to the world around them. His curriculum focused on a belief that the adults in children's lives should guide them to develop a sense of themselves as complete individuals and a connection to nature, the spiritual world, other children, and all humanity (Corbett 1988). Froebel's original geometric shapes consisted of cubes, cylinders, spheres, rectangles, and columns, and their use was scripted. Children were directed to create patterns and designs using symmetry, balance, and proportion. Children were taught counting, fractions, and other mathematical knowledge, such as the names of the geometric shapes and the meaning of such terms as *diagonal, vertical,* and *horizontal* by using the shapes. These concepts and terms are found today in many state and federal standards. Open-ended discovery encouraging the use of imagination and creativity through play was not a part of this curriculum, but the use of objects for children to manipulate set a new direction in the education of young children.

At the turn of the twentieth century, a woman named Carolyn Pratt created her entire classroom curriculum around the use of small pieces of wood found in waste bins, and the rest is history. As time

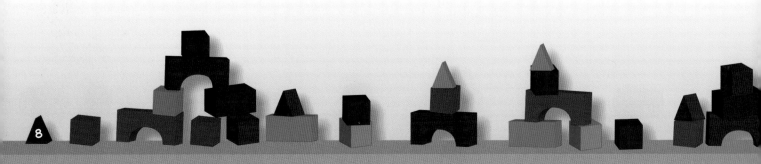

went on, Carolyn Pratt began to have very specific blocks made for the children in her school, City and Country School. These pieces of wood, patterned after the gifts created by Frederick Froebel and described in his book *The Education of Man,* which was published in 1826, are the same kind of blocks still used today by children in programs around the world.

Carolyn Pratt's focus was for children to create meaningful educational experiences using construction and dramatic play. She believed that combining these two play experiences would help children form a foundation from which all early learning could be built. She believed that through the school curriculum, children could learn the knowledge that would support the creation of a society that would work together for the betterment of all. Carolyn Pratt's educational insights continue today to impact early-childhood classrooms across the world. Numerous people have tried to change her standards and design blocks all the same shape and size or color them with paint. While these other construction materials add to the play choices of young children, none have taken the place of the original shapes and sizes designed by Carolyn Pratt.

Maria Montessori used wooden blocks and other materials children could manipulate in the "work" experiences she designed to prepare them for success as adults. She was concerned about the lack of education provided for poorer children and children with disabilities she found on the streets and in the asylums of Rome. Like Froebel and Pratt, Montessori believed that the education of the youngest children held the key to the development of a better society. She used materials that allowed children to develop knowledge at their own pace while using as many of their senses as possible. "From the hands to the mind" is an expression often used in Montessori training. "The materials used by the senses are a doorway to the mind" (O'Brien 1998, 5). Today, brain research supports her work. We now know that the more of the five senses of seeing, hearing, touching, smelling, and tasting are involved in an experience, the more children remember and learn.

Regarding the learning environments designed for our youngest children, perhaps Jean Piaget said it best:

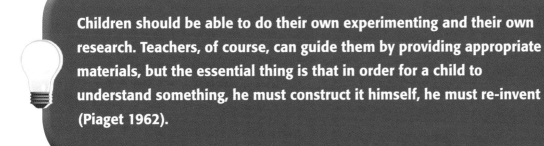

Children should be able to do their own experimenting and their own research. Teachers, of course, can guide them by providing appropriate materials, but the essential thing is that in order for a child to understand something, he must construct it himself, he must re-invent (Piaget 1962).

LET'S BUILD: Strong Foundations in Language, Math, and Social Skills

What is Play?

One reason parents and early-childhood educators have moved away from play and toward worksheets and memorized facts is because they do not understand play. In our work-oriented society, play is often viewed as a waste of time, and many parents do not want their children to play with paint or make mudpies. They send their children to preschool neatly dressed and expect them to return home looking much the same. As adults, it is hard to remember what we did as three- and four-year-olds; elementary and high-school experiences are easier to remember and often blur the memories of our younger years. Memories of desks, tests, worksheets, drill, and recess fill our memories and confuse the delights we felt during play as young children and can influence the schedules we plan for young children. Because so many children between the ages of birth and five spend most of each day in child care, it is essential that the adults in these settings understand how children grow and learn and not fill children's days with worksheets, short recess times, and circle time activities filled with drill and memorization.

Time for Play

It is important to make sure that children have ample time to play. Research and theory show that well-planned play experiences that are supported by adults who understand how young children grow and develop will provide opportunities for children to discover knowledge and develop the skills needed for later school success.

The Characteristics of Play

Many books have been written about play and its importance in the developing lives of children. Stuart Brown and his colleague Christopher Vaughn in their book, *Play: How It Shapes The Brain, Opens the Imagination, and Invigorates the Soul* (2009), describe not only how play contributes to the positive development of children, but also how playing in childhood impacts the success, physical health, and joy in the lives of these children when they are adults. Brown and Vaughn's work shows that adults

who engaged in dramatic and construction play as children are better problem solvers and creative thinkers as adults. Brown lists the following properties of play:

- ❏ Apparently purposeless (done for its own sake)
- ❏ Voluntary (do it because you want to)
- ❏ Inherently attractive (just fun)
- ❏ Free from time (lose the sense of time)
- ❏ Diminished consciousness of self (don't worry about how we are doing)
- ❏ Improvisational potential (open to new ways of doing)
- ❏ Continuation desire (pleasure keeps us playing)

When you watch children at play, all of these characteristics are evident. Children who have developmentally appropriate opportunities to play are engaged (their minds are busily at work) and they are happy. Whether playing alone or with others, their play reflects their ability to focus and create, to problem solve, and to think critically.

> **Children love to play, but it isn't always easy to see the learning opportunities when we see children engaged in play. The challenge for us is to understand *what* children are doing when they are playing and *how* play behaviors lead to learning.**

The Value of Play

Children love to play, but it isn't always easy to see the learning opportunities when we see children engaged in play. The challenge for us is to understand **what** children are doing when they are playing and **how** play behaviors lead to learning. Although play is almost always a valuable learning

11

experience for children, play can also meet learning standards and learning objectives. Standards are here to stay; they are shaping curriculums in programs serving our youngest children. If play is what we, as early educators, want to protect and provide in early-education and care programs, we must be able to communicate a clear understanding of how to support children's play experiences and what these experiences contribute to the development of young children in a way that can be easily understood by parents and early educastors.

The Categories of Play

Research and theory focus on the kinds of play, the value of play, and the stages of children's development that can be assessed by observing children's behavior during play and by what they create. Once you better understand the facets of play, you will be able to value it, provide materials to support it, and comfortably afford ample time for children to pursue it to its full extent.

The play of children can be divided into the following four categories (Piaget 1962; Erikson 1977; Smilansky 1968; Wolfgang 1992):

1. SENSORIMOTOR PLAY:

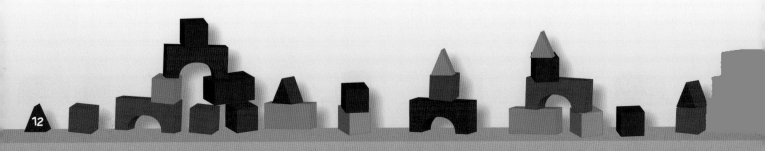

2. DRAMATIC PLAY:

Microdramatic

Macrodramatic

3. CONSTRUCTION PLAY:

Fluid

Structured

4. GAMES WITH RULES

Sensorimotor Play

We all engage in sensorimotor play. Piaget (1962) used the term to describe the behaviors he observed in babies. They use their senses of seeing, hearing, touching, tasting, and smelling to learn about objects in their world. As children grow and develop, they continue to engage in sensorimotor play as they strive to understand and control the materials they encounter. The following definitions of sensorimotor play have been used first in research and then in helping parents and early educators understand the behaviors of young children (Hanline, Milton, and Phelps 2008):

SENSORIMOTOR 1 The child is engaged in what Piaget called primary circular reactions. Only the child's body is involved. Toys and objects are not used. The child splashes her hands in the water in the water table or runs her hands through the sand in the sandbox.

SENSORIMOTOR 2 The child is engaged in repetition of an action using an object. The same action is repeated again and again to recreate a visual, auditory, or tactile event. Piaget called this a secondary circular reaction. The child bangs two blocks together again and again, enjoying the sound, or dips a colander into the water table and watches the water cascade back into the table.

SENSORIMOTOR 3 The child is engaged in the repetition of a simple cause-and-effect sequence in which a goal is chosen. The child stacks a few blocks and knocks the structure down or pours water into a pitcher with a goal of filling it up.

SENSORIMOTOR 4 In this level of sensorimotor behavior, the child engages in trial-and-error experimentation. The child stacks two blocks that are the same size and shape, then tries to fit a larger, different shape on the top. Because the last block continues to fall off, the child uses blocks that are other sizes and shapes until the tower stands.

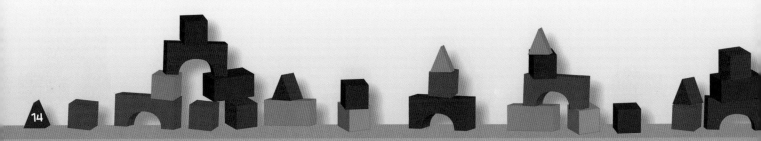

Dramatic Play

The second kind of play discussed in the literature is dramatic play, which is often called fantasy, make-believe, imaginative, or symbolic play. In this kind of play, the child can take on a role and enter a world he creates. During dramatic play experiences, the child can change reality to fit his image of what should or did happen. For example, the child who wants a new puppy will pretend he is a puppy and run around the playground barking (macrodramatic play), or he will play with the small dog figures in a basket in the block area (microdramatic play). Through his play, he can fulfill his desire to own a puppy.

Construction Play

Dr. Charles Wolfgang (1992) studied the play of children throughout his career. His work provides a method of thinking about the kinds of materials children use in construction play experiences. He placed the materials that children can use in construction/constructive play along a continuum from the most fluid (water) to the most structured (puzzles). This third kind of play allows children's play to have an intentional result (product). Construction play occurs after children move beyond engaging in sensorimotor play. The following list includes some of the possible materials that can be offered for construction-play experiences:

Fluid materials do not have a predetermined shape. The fluid nature of these materials supports the sensorimotor needs of children. As children learn to control the materials, they begin a journey that takes them from smearing and scribbling to realistic representations that can be explained by descriptions offered by the child. Fluid materials are vital play materials for older infants, toddlers, and preschoolers. Water, sand, and paint will keep young children focused for long periods of time as they strive to understand and control them.

As children learn to control materials, they are learning to control themselves. The ability to focus and control one's behavior is one of the foundational tools needed for success (Galinsky 2010). As children play at a water table with funnels, turkey basters, plastic tubing of different sizes, and other tools, they are engaging in scientific discovery. All domains of development can be supported through such experiences (Drew, et al 2008). With appropriate teacher support (scaffolding), children can discover and begin to understand many concepts that will support later schoolwork.

Structured materials have a predetermined shape that controls how children can use the materials and

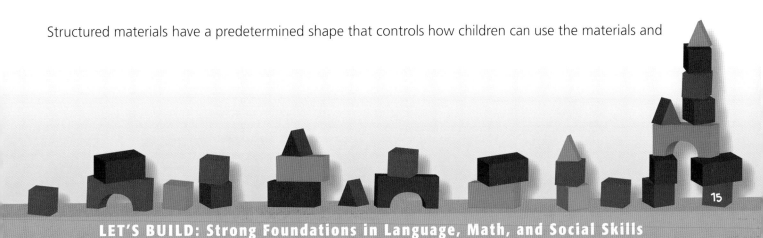

what they can create. For example, children can only make enclosures with Lincoln Logs; children must place puzzle pieces into the positions that they were made to fit. Construction play is also described as organized play that is goal-oriented. In construction/constructive play, children use materials to build something (Johnson, Christie, and Wardle 2005).

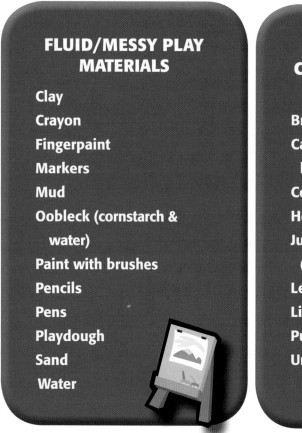

FLUID/MESSY PLAY MATERIALS

Clay
Crayon
Fingerpaint
Markers
Mud
Oobleck (cornstarch & water)
Paint with brushes
Pencils
Pens
Playdough
Sand
Water

STRUCTURED/ CONSTRUCTION PLAY MATERIALS

Bristle blocks
Cardboard and vinyl blocks
Colored blocks
Hollow blocks
Junk materials (Drew and Rankin 2004)
Legos
Lincoln Logs
Puzzles
Unit blocks

Games with Rules

The fourth kind of play, games with rules, requires that children understand the point of view of another, in Piaget's words, "to take the perspective of another" (1962). Children must also be able to follow a set of standard rules and understand the concept of win or lose. These cognitive abilities are not usually developed until children reach the age of six, seven, or beyond. Games with rules include baseball, football, and board games. Anyone who has played these games with a young child knows they have difficulty following the rules, waiting a turn, and losing (Wolfgang and Wolfgang 1992).

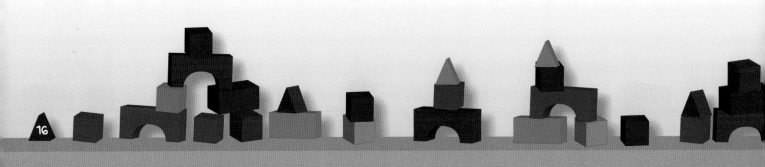

Learning Reading & Writing Through Play

Through sensorimotor, dramatic, and construction play experiences, children learn to understand their world and to reproduce their ideas and experiences in their play behaviors and in the intentional results (products) of their play.

Children from different cultures and different countries around the world demonstrate the same stages of play as they journey toward using their abstract symbol system for reading and writing. Children begin with smears and scribbles and then they create more and more realistic drawings and paintings. They imitate behaviors done to them and around them, developing the ability to play with other children and the capacity to retell whole stories about events they have experienced and things they have imagined.

LET'S BUILD: Strong Foundations in Language, Math, and Social Skills

Children build with construction materials such as blocks, carrying them around at first and developing into builders of elaborate structures that have symmetry and reflect an intricate balance as children become four- and five-year-olds. As children become more mature in their play, they will build a structure or structures alone or with other children and move freely between dramatic and construction play. Piaget suggested that during construction play, children move between play and work. Creating structures requires many of the skills needed in work: having a predetermined idea of what is to be built, staying focused and following the task from beginning to end, and discussing the structure and its use with peers and adults (Piaget 1962).

As children develop the ability to create realistic representations in their play (at the easel, drawing, and with blocks), they begin to play with the letters, numbers, and then words of their language. Through play, each child recapitulates the journey cultures have taken as they have progressed to the creation of a written language. This is called the journey from "symbol to sign." **_Sign_** is the written symbol system of a culture and is abstract. The word _cat_ doesn't look like a cat. Before the interest in and the ability to use such an abstract system, children begin to symbolically represent their world in realistic drawings, paintings, and structures. In a block structure, a house looks like a house; and in a drawing, a cat looks like a cat. Pictures are representations. Signs are representations also, but they are abstract (Wolfgang and Wolfgang 2005).

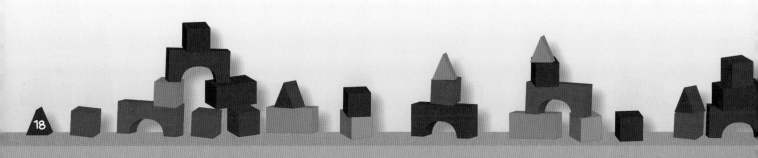

Weikart's (1970) *The Cognitively Oriented Curriculum* is designed around this journey that each child makes from manipulating and experimenting with materials (sensorimotor) to reproducing an experience through play by drawing pictures, building structures with blocks, reenacting the experience in micro- and macrodramatic play, using language to describe and explain, and finally, to using written words (sign). Weikart's curriculum takes the child from an experience with the actual object to the picture of the object and then to the written word for the object.

As children progress from sensorimotor play alone as infants and toddlers to symbolic players with other children at ages three, four, five, and six, their play becomes more mature and purposeful. According to research conducted by Bodrova and Leong (2004), this level of play can be observed when the following are present:

1. There is an imaginary situation.

2. Explicit roles are assigned.

3. There are implicit rules that govern the interactions.

Construction play experiences are important ingredients in a quality early-childhood environment. Fluid construction play can be messy, but its open-ended qualities allow children great opportunities to make their own creations and discover the qualities of different materials as children develop self-control. Structured construction play can be noisy, and the challenge to offer enough pieces to encourage and sustain children's in-depth play is sometimes daunting, but its significance to the development of math, science, and social knowledge is invaluable

Supporting Children's Play Experiences

If young children are to be supported in their development of the skills and knowledge they will need for lifelong learning, they must have early childhood experiences that are planned and intentionally implemented. The environments in which children play should support an appropriate intensity and density of play opportunities.

Intensity and Density of Play Experiences

The concept of **_intensity_** refers to the amount of time that children are allowed to experience materials and engage in the three kinds of play. If children are supported in their journey from the creation of symbols in their play to the use of letters and words, they must have opportunities to practice and explore every day. The amount of time during each day and throughout the year equals the intensity of experience (CCCRT 2002; Hanline, Milton, and Phelps 2001).

Intensity—The amount of time the child is allowed to experience the three kinds of play during each day and throughout the year

Children love novelty. Because their brains are wired to observe what is typical and look for the different or novel, it is important to provide interesting new ways for children to practice skills and discover knowledge. Structured construction opportunities using recycled materials, hammers, nails, and pieces of wood as well as different kinds of blocks provide **_density_**. The addition of new props in the block area supports the play of new dramatic scenarios. Children need to build, to create their own symbolic representations, so offer the media children need that provide new opportunities to explore, discover, and create.

Density—The variety of ways each kind of play is presented for children to experience.

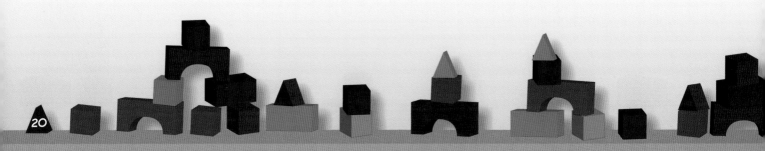

Structured Construction Play

Structured construction play materials have a predetermined shape that controls how the material can be used. There are many different types of structured construction materials available. When you purchase structured construction materials, pay close attention to the open-endedness of the material and how much of children's imagination can be supported through play with the material. Many construction materials look cute with faces, letters, and numbers painted on them; however, the very best materials are unpainted pieces of hardwood blocks in numerous shape choices.

Natural hardwood blocks are called unit blocks and follow the original designs created by Carolyn Pratt. Recognizing and knowing the names of these geometric shapes will contribute to children's later school success in math and science. The chart on page 22 shows the shapes and names. When you interact and talk with children about their constructions, it is important to use these names to discuss and describe children's creations.

Unit blocks were designed to be equivalent. A double unit is the same as two units and a quad is the same as four units. The dimensions and shapes of these blocks provide children with opportunities to develop logical-mathematical knowledge (DeVries and Kohlberg 1987).

Sets of unit blocks can be purchased through many companies that provide materials for early-childhood classrooms. A basic set often consists of approximately 100 pieces of 28 shapes. Research and observations of young children using unit blocks (CCCRT 2002) shows that a child who is beginning to build symbolically with blocks will use between 50 and 100 pieces in a structure. **When children are limited in the number and variety of block pieces available for their play, the possibilities for children's development is limited. Ideally, the number of pieces of blocks provided should determine the number of children using an area for block play.** A block area providing construction opportunities for four preschool children should have

UNIT BLOCK SHAPES

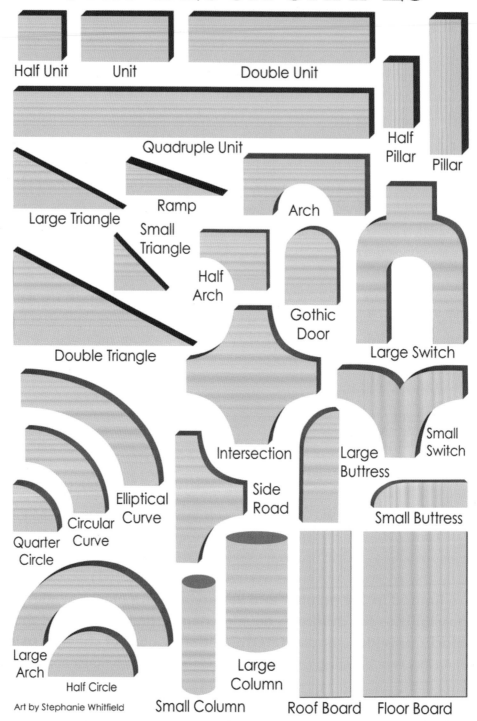

Half Unit

Unit

Double Unit

Quadruple Unit

Half Pillar

Pillar

Large Triangle

Ramp

Small Triangle

Arch

Half Arch

Gothic Door

Large Switch

Double Triangle

Intersection

Large Buttress

Small Switch

Elliptical Curve

Circular Curve

Side Road

Small Buttress

Quarter Circle

Large Arch

Half Circle

Small Column

Large Column

Roof Board

Floor Board

Art by Stephanie Whitfield

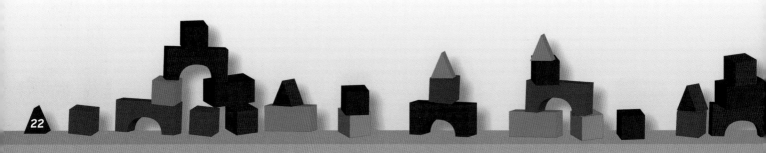

a minimum of 400 pieces of blocks in 28 shapes. Children in kindergarten and elementary school should have access to approximately 200 pieces of blocks per child. These amounts greatly exceed previous recommendations (Wellhousen and Kieff 2001; Stanton and Weisberg 1996). However, the following pictures taken of structures of three-, four-, and five-year-old children support these new recommendations. Children who created the pictured structures have had daily opportunities to use unit blocks in a block area that has more than 300 blocks per child. While many might consider this excessive, the structures created by these children are very elaborate, involve a time commitment from children, and demonstrate children's symbolic ability at the time the structure was completed.

The children who built the structures pictured were first introduced to play with unit blocks when they were eighteen months old. Many adults prefer to use of vinyl and cardboard construction materials with toddlers, but they can learn to

69 BLOCKS USED

72 BLOCKS USED

98 BLOCKS USED

use these blocks safely and well with appropriate adult guidance and support (scaffolding).

Hollow blocks are a larger version of the unit block. They are usually made from hardwood and in a few shapes such as squares, rectangles, and triangles. Several companies now offer a mini version of these blocks to support the play of toddlers and young three's. These larger blocks allow children to create structures that they can fit inside of (macrospheric), which provide broader opportunities to engage socially with other children. Mildred Parten (1932) calls this kind of social interaction *cooperative play.* Cooperative play occurs when children come together and plan to build something, and once it is built, they take on roles and engage in dramatic play. Many times children will use the large hollow blocks to build the framework and the unit blocks for the decorations or small additions.

Blocks should be organized on shelving that is easily reached by young children. How blocks are placed onto the shelving is very important. The ability to group the same objects together and see connections between objects is vital to higher-level thinking skills, creativity, and problem solving (Galinsky 2010). Each kind of block should be classified, and seriation of the shapes should be a prominent feature when planning the organization of the blocks on shelving. For example, all the cylinders should be placed together and organized from the largest to the smallest or the tallest to the shortest. This organization clearly demonstrates to children the concept of seriation, which they experience as they move the blocks to and from

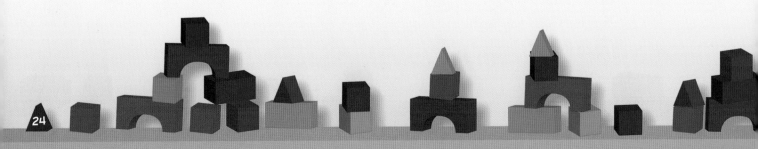

the shelving. Children may not be able to explain seriation, but they are using it, and when you use the correct language to describe the children's behavior, you are expanding their receptive language. Research has shown that this knowledge is retrieved as children age and move into educational experiences that require higher-level thinking skills and mathematical knowledge (Wolfgang, Stannard, and Jones 2001).

Place labels onto the back of the shelves or onto the front edge so children can use the labels to match the blocks to the shapes pictured. You can make block labels by taking close pictures of the block shapes placed onto a piece of dark colored paper. Laminating the pictures after printing will result in sturdy labels that will last.

As children return blocks to the shelves, help them find the correct space by suggesting that they "read" the labels on the shelving. Of course they will be reading pictures of the blocks not the words for the blocks, but this is a symbolic matching exercise and helps children begin to understand the meaning of reading. Clearly print the name for each block below the picture, and over time, children will begin to match the picture and the word. Children in the Creative Pre-School have said, "I read the shelf all by myself and found out where the block lived." Remember that Vygotsky (1967) believed that during play children could place themselves above their actual developmental level. Children must believe they can read long before they actually read. When block shelves are labeled with pictures and the words for the shapes, children can see the actual block shape, match it to the picture, and later use the words to lead them to the correct area of organization. The labeling of the shelving provides children with a daily opportunity to practice the journey from symbol to sign. Children must have direct experiences with objects and people in their world in order to develop clear understandings (Piaget 1962; Weikart et al 1970; Biber et al 1971; Wolfgang and Wolfgang 1992, 1995; Galinsky 2010). Direct experiences with objects that allow children opportunities to classify and organize materials can lead to children making unusual connections between these objects. Teachers must be alert to the creative attempts children make to change the use and purpose of objects.

Place a poster with the block shapes and names near the block area so the adults and children in the classroom can see the proper names. Understanding the names for the block shapes and hearing these names used to describe children's constructions helps them develop mathematical knowledge (Hanline, Milton, and Phelps 2009; Geist 2001; Gregory, Kim, and Whiren 2003).

The Structured Construction Play Area

When areas for building are clearly defined, children can see where the construction area begins and ends. This helps them move with confidence around the structures of others as they move to and from the shelves of blocks. To create individual building sites, cut a 4' x 8' x 1" piece of marine-grade plywood into geometric shapes. This plywood costs a little more, but it is less likely to splinter and lends itself to sanding and repainting and years of use. Two pieces of 4' x 8' plywood can be cut into squares, triangles, and rectangles without any waste of material.

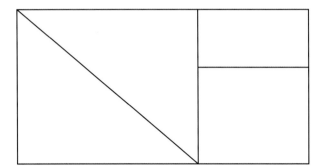 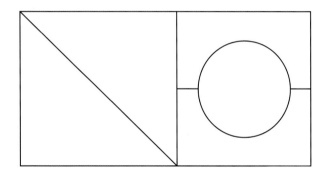

These shapes can be stacked when not in use to provide open floor space and stacked on top of several large hollow blocks to create instant tables for children to work at as they sit on the floor. Carpet in the block area helps contain the noise created by enthusiastic building, and these shapes provide a firm surface on which to build. Tape on a carpet is not recommended as it leaves a glue residue that will eventually result in dark marks on the carpet.

The construction area should be large enough to provide each child building in the area approximately 20 to 25 square feet. This construction area can easily double as a space for circle or group time when not used as a construction area. Although this double use prevents structures from being saved for future building, most classrooms do not have the footage to allow structures to be saved.

Children's constructions should not be built within 18" of the shelves. This allotment of floor space in front of the shelves allows children to freely move to and from the shelves as they choose the blocks for their structure.

Standards

Many state standards list as learning goals the names of geometric two- and three-dimensional shapes, positional terms, as well as mathematical knowledge, such as one-to-one correspondence, creating patterns, putting sets together and taking them apart. The National Association for the Education of Young Children (NAEYC) and The National Council of Teachers of Mathematics (NCTM) adopted a joint position statement in 2002 that was revised in 2010. This position statement is an excellent guide for determining what to do to promote the development of quality experiences in early childhood environments. The educational expectations described in state standards and the NAEYC/NCTM position statement can all be used to create quality experiences using blocks.

The following taken from the position statement (2002, 2010) suggests five content areas that should be embedded in daily natural experiences that present themselves during the routines and play opportunities in an early childhood environment:

1. NUMBER AND OPERATIONS

2. GEOMETRY AND SPATIAL SENSE

3. MEASUREMENT

4. PATTERN/ALGEBRAIC THINKING

5. DISPLAYING AND ANALYZING DATA

While these terms may cause some early childhood educators to be anxious about their own math ability and, therefore, their ability to support the development of this content knowledge in their environments, the actual implementation is easy and simply means being aware of opportunities when working with young children.

Numbers and Operations

There are many opportunities each day to explore this concept. Counting cups, blocks, and the number of children present, and asking "how many" questions. Do we have enough? Are there more than we need?

Geometry and Spatial Sense

For children to learn this concept, you must know the names of two-dimensional and three-dimensional shapes and involve children in discovering shapes that present themselves in materials, buildings, pictures, and other objects in the environment. Daily opportunities to explore shapes and discuss their features should be provided. The block area is a wonderful site for these discussions.

Measurement

Throughout the day, use comparing words as you model and discuss measuring things. "Is this block heavier, longer, or thicker than this one?" "If we use Charlie's shoe to measure the length of this table, how many shoes long do you estimate that it will be?" (nonstandard measurement)

Pattern/Algebraic Thinking

Notice and describe patterns in the environment and patterns children make using materials. Learning the skills of recognizing patterns and creating patterns is vital for reading, math, and critical thinking. Materials that allow children to practice pattern making is one small part of this concept. The world is filled with patterns that adults can help children discover. For example, create, notice, and describe patterns with different colored chairs placed around a table. Discuss the patterns in math experiences, such as when zero is added to a number it always equals that number or that when you add one to a number it moves one up the number line.

Displaying and Analyzing Data

To help children explore and learn about this concept, engage them in organizing, comparing, and contrasting groups of objects. For example, summarizing the number of sunny, rainy, or cloudy days on a chart is a way to create simple tables and graphs. Placing the different shapes of blocks in lines to see which shape was used most, which shape was used least. Was the same amount of any shapes used?

A more knowledgeable peer or adult who can describe and discuss the experiences with children helps them understand and explore their experiences so they receive the full benefit of the experiences. Children depend on social exchanges to receive the information needed to make new connections involving ideas and objects they are working with.

Through social and language interactions, older and more experienced members of a community teach younger and less-experienced members the skills, values, and knowledge needed to be productive members of that community (Harry Daniels, An Introduction to Vygotsky 2005).

LET'S BUILD: Strong Foundations in Language, Math, and Social Skills

Rich, learning-filled experiences and expanded knowledge result when a knowledgeable peer or adult interacts with children before, during, and after new experiences.

THE FOLLOWING LIST OF TERMS SHOULD BE USED IN EVERYDAY EXPERIENCES IN THE BLOCK AREA:

Arch	Curve	Horizontal	Perimeter	Stable
Around	Cylinder	Huge	Perspective	Structural
Attic	Depth	Inside	Pillar	integrity
Balance	Diagonal	Interior	Pinnacle	Support
Base	Double	Landscape	Plank	Switch
Basement	Ellipse	Large, largest	Platform	Symmetrical
Beside	Equivalent	Length	Porch	Symmetry
Between	Even	Level	Proportion	Tall
Board	Exterior	Mini, miniature	Quadruple	Tapered
Bottom	Fence	Moat	Quarter	Tiny
Bridge	Floor	Mortar	Ramp	Top
Castle	Fortress	Number	Right angle	Tower
Ceiling	Foundation	words 1–100	Roman arch	Towering
Circle	Gate	Numerals 1–10	Roof	Unit
Cone	Geometric	Obelisk	Shore up	Unstable
Corner	Half	Odd	Short	Vertical
Courtyard	Height	Outside	Small, smallest	Width
			Square	

The block area offers unique opportunities for teachers to embed math and science knowledge and information in children's experiences and to support children's acquisition of new vocabulary and language skills as they play. In addition, when children move about the block area, they are learning to consider the perspective of others and how to move their bodies in space.

BLOCK PLAY PROVIDES OPPORTUNITIES FOR CHILDREN TO DEVELOP:

Peer interaction skills

Communication abilities

Expanded vocabulary

Fine and gross motor strength and coordination

Mathematical and geometric concepts

Symbolic thinking

Topological knowledge

Visual discrimination skills

—Supported through the work of Guanella (1934),
Reifel (1982), and Phelps and Hanline (1999)

Become familiar with the standards for your state and the expectations for children's learning in the NAEYC/NCTM position statement so you can plan specific experiences that offer children the opportunities they need to discover new knowledge and develop these early skills and knowledge.

Scaffolding the Block Play Experience

Research and theory have shown that children need opportunities to formulate new ideas and time to develop in-depth aspect to their play. Whether your program has a large area for blocks or an area where only two children can play at a time, books, pictures, trips, and visitors can help children develop new ideas and learn new vocabulary that will support all of their play throughout the early childhood environment.

In order to move beyond "just play" and the continuous repetition of play themes, children need the following (Smilansky 1968, 1990; CCCRT 2002):

❑ A shared background of experience

❑ Enough time to bring the construction of their structure to completion and move into micro-dramatic play alone or with other children.

❑ Enough pieces of blocks to build their structure, enough space to build, and enough micro- and macrodramatic play props to support the later play. Microplay props are miniature props such as animals and people. Macroplay props are costumes that allow children to become the people or animals they are pretending to be. These terms come out of the work of Erik Erikson (1977).

Microplay props are miniature props such as animals and people. Macroplay props are costumes that allow the child to become the person or animal they are pretending to be. These terms come out of the work of Erik Erikson (1977).

❒ Adult interaction to expand their vocabulary and concepts, support their ideas, and model appropriate social interaction (scaffolding).

Scaffolding is a term often mistakenly attached to Vygotsky's work. He never used the term *scaffolding* but discussed the importance of the "zone of proximal development." **Scaffolding** uses this same construct and means that the teacher provides children with new information about how to use materials and introduces new vocabulary and concepts. Because she understands each child's interests and development, she can provide support for children's play that is neither overwhelming nor simplistic.

You can use four scaffolding components to ensure that children have not only quality block-play experiences, but also quality experiences for all centers. These components are scaffolding:

1. The play environment,

2. The pre-play experiences,

3. The individual child's play experience, and

4. The post-play experiences (CCCRT, 2002).

Although each component is a distinct entity, it is also possible to blend them into an integrated meaningful experience for the group and for each individual child.

Scaffolding the Play Environment

❒ Pre-organize the construction environment with building areas clearly denoted

❒ Plan for intensity and density of the construction experience (See page 20 for more information about intensity and density of play experiences.)

❒ Arrange the construction environment to support positive social interactions

❒ Allow access to a **minimum** of 100 (200 for kindergarteners) natural-color unit blocks for each child in the group

❒ Have sets of colored blocks classified by color for decorating completed constructions

❏ Have a variety of micro- and macrodramatic play props available to expand the construction experience into dramatic play, for example:

- ◯ People

  - Cultural diversity
  - Role diversity
  - Age diversity

- ◯ Disabilities positively depicted

- ◯ Vehicles

  - Automobiles
  - Farm equipment
  - Other modes of transportation—These should be small. Large vehicles are best used outdoors.

- ◯ Animal Families

  - Farm Forest, and Jungle (zoo)—Families of animals support less aggressive play. When only one animal per species is provided and the animals are depicted in an aggressive stance, aggressive play is supported.

In addition to materials listed, small carpet pieces, trees, shells, colored stones, and so on can be provided, which will allow children to decorate their structures, enhancing the quality of the structures as well as supporting the possibilities for dramatic play.

Have literacy materials available for children to use, such as coffee-table picture books, children's books, pictures of buildings, paper, pencils, markers, and other materials.

Scaffolding the Pre-Construction Play Experience

❑ Read a book that sets the tone for the construction experience.

❑ Incorporate new vocabulary and demonstrate concepts that focus on building structures.

❑ Discuss ideas for the construction play experience.

❑ Provide children with opportunities for successful social interactions by allocating enough space and materials.

❑ Discuss rules and expectations for the construction experience.

❑ Design and implement an orderly transition to play.

Scaffolding the Individual Child's Construction Play Experience

❑ Give each child ample time (minimum of 60 minutes of actual construction and playtime), floor space (20–25 square feet per child), and materials to complete his or her construction.

❑ Enhance and extend language through questioning and discussion of the construction activity.

❑ Model appropriate communication through individual conversations as each child builds.

❑ Increase socialization opportunities through support of peer interactions.

❑ Observe and document each child's construction development and progress.

Scaffolding the Post-Construction Play Experience

❑ Recall and review the construction experience, allowing children to share their accomplishments.

❑ Use cleanup as a positive learning experience by encouraging children to classify, seriate, and generally organize the construction environment.

Cleanup

Children come into the early childhood environment with a preconceived idea or perhaps no idea at all about what **cleanup** means. Putting away materials is an important opportunity to teach classification skills and responsibility. Teach children what **cleanup** means and why it is important. Spend time teaching children how to reorganize the play space. If the materials in the room are classified and organized well, children can easily put them in their proper places. When children say, "But I didn't play there," explain that living in a group setting means that the responsibility of the environment belongs to the group. One suggestion is to gather children into a circle before cleanup time and assign groups of children for each task. Each group can include an experienced cleaner with a less accomplished one, using peer modeling. If two teachers are present, one should start a story or music circle once approximately half the children have completed their tasks. This helps prevent a "storm" of unwanted behavior. Transitions are very difficult for many children, making longer periods of focused activity important. A well-scaffolded, structured construction-play experience should allow one-and–one-half hours for the four scaffolding components (see page 33) to be accomplished. This provides enough time for new ideas to be offered, time for children to create and use their structures, time for the adults to observe and scaffold each child's play, and time to share the morning experiences and implement a useful clean-up experience.

Scaffolding Children's Construction Play

Research has substantiated the importance of adult scaffolding during block play (Gregory, Kim, and Whiren 2003). Just standing around is not enough. You must engage with children, enhancing the building experience by following their interest in the structures, embedding new vocabulary when appropriate, and asking open-ended questions.

You can use children's books as well as adult picture books (fiction and nonfiction) to help children with ideas for their constructions. Children are interested in adult picture books of bridges, tall buildings, castles, and other constructions as well as colorful pictures of structures from around the world, which can be found in calendars and magazines.

A digital camera is another great tool for enhancing the block/construction area. Around any town or city there are interesting buildings displaying geometric shapes. Take pictures of interesting structures locally and as you travel. Laminate printed, page-sized (8½" x 11") pictures of buildings, punch a hole into each picture, and connect the picture into a set with a metal ring.

Using literacy materials such as paper, pens, books, and markers in the block area supports children's emergent literacy attempts as they create signs for their structures, draw pictures of buildings they are thinking about constructing, or look at pictures and books that interest them.

The use of literacy materials to enrich the block-building experience has been found to have long-term positive effects on the reading and math abilities of children with and without disabilities (Hanline, Milton, and Phelps 2009).

The four scaffolding components (scaffolding the play environment, the pre-construction play experience, the individual child's contraction play experience, and the post-construction play experience) when implemented in an early childhood environment provide a framework that ensures that children have enough materials to support the three kinds of play; that they know the expectations for the play; that their play activities are observed and supported; and that they are provided time to review and evaluate their experience.

Children's Books that Support Children's Construction Play

The following is a short list of some children's books that can be placed into or near the block-building area. These books, along with adult pictures books, will provide children with construction ideas. Add your own favorite books to the block area.

Alphabet Under Construction by Denise Fleming (2006)—This colorful book features a hard-working mouse constructing a wild, artistic alphabet.

B Is for Bulldozer: A Construction ABC by June Sobel and illustrated by Melissa Iwai (2003)—This colorful book uses simple drawings of machines to support the introduction of alphabet letters, A to Z.

Block City by Robert Louis Stevenson and illustrated by Daniel Kirk (2005)—The illustrator has transformed this famous, classic poem into a delightful picture book that tells the story of how a boy creates a stately kingdom out of his blocks and other toys.

Brooklyn Bridge by Lynn Curlee (2001)—This historical children's book is illustrated in soft, colorful, realistic drawings that tell the story of the building of this great bridge.

Building a House by Byron Barton (1981)—This little book takes children from the initial digging of the hole for the basement to the step-by-step completion of the house. The use of simple words and pictures makes this book real for young builders.

Castle by Christopher Gravett (2008)—This book is a resource for discussing castles, including the how and the why they were built. It is not a storybook. The illustrations consist of realistic drawings as well as photographs.

Castles and Fortresses by Robin S. Oggins (1998)—This book for adults consists of full-page, color photographs of castles and fortresses that have been built around the world. Each photograph is supported by a description of how and why the construction was undertaken.

Changes, Changes by Pat Hutchins (1971)—*Changes, Changes* is a wordless picture book about two wooden people who use their block shapes to create answers to the problems they face in their changing block world.

The Construction Alphabet Book by Jerry Pallotta and Rob Boister (2006)—Children love large machines and this book presents each letter of the alphabet, A through Z, by a piece of realistically drawn equipment that can be found at construction sites.

Construction Countdown by K. C. Olson and David Gordon (2004)—This is a counting book that uses construction vehicles as the objects that are counted. The illustrations are colorful and attract the attention of young listeners.

Digging Machines written by staff of the Fog City Press (2008)—This book is filled with vocabulary such as *scoop, drill, haul,* and *crush.* Diggers are important machines, as are many others used in the construction of large buildings.

A House Is a House for Me by Mary Ann Hoberman (1978)—Using detailed colorful illustrations and rhyme, this delightful book provides a catalog of places where animals and people live.

The House That Jack Built by Diana Mayo (2001)—Delightful colorful drawings depict this revisit of the traditional rhyme.

Houses and Homes by Ann Morris and Ken Heyman (1992)—This book shows in beautiful color photographs places where people live.

How a House Is Built by Gail Gibbons (1990, 1996)—This simple picture book describes how workers such as plumbers, surveyors, and others use their skills to build a house.

I Want to Be a Builder by Dan Liebman (2003)—This book is part of a series of paperback publications that focus on occupations. The colorful full-page photographs picture the work of a builder. The opening page, however, pictures a young child learning to become a builder by constructing with blocks.

Iggy Peck, Architect by Andrea Beaty (2010)—Iggy loves to build and finds many different materials with which to build. This book uses rhyme and cartoon-like illustrations to tell a very funny story about an unusual boy.

Katy and the Big Snow by Virginia Lee Burton (1943)—This old book shows how Katy, a helpful large red bulldozer, helps the city during a big snow. The illustrations are simple, cartoon-like, but delightful. This book has stood the test of time.

Lighthouses: A Pictorial History of Lighthouses Around the World by Leo Marriott (1999)—This is an adult picture book of large, colorful photographs of lighthouses. Each lighthouse photograph is followed by a description of where it is located and how/why it was built.

The Little House by Virginia Lee Burton (1942)—This great old picture book tells the story of a little house that becomes misplaced by the expansion of the city. It is a wonderful story for discussing the differences between city and country life. The seasons are also depicted in delightful pictures showing the little house as time goes by.

The Little Red Lighthouse and the Great Gray Bridge, restored edition by Hildegarde Swift (2003)—The little red lighthouse feels misplaced as the great towering bridge is built over the top of it. This is a great story the can be used to emphasize how small things can be of help. Bigger is not always the only answer.

Mike Mulligan and His Steam Shovel by Virginia Lee Burton (1939)—This old book shows how the basement is built for a building and a disaster is averted through creative thinking on the part of Mike Mulligan.

Richard Scarry's Busy, Busy Town by Richard Scarry (2000)—This book is filled with intricate cartoon-like illustrations that show the people who live and work in a city. Children will enjoy looking for the workers (personified animals) from picture to picture.

Shapes, Shapes, Shapes by Tana Hoban (1996)—This wordless picture book presents actual pictures of everyday objects depicting shapes such as circles, squares, triangles, and ovals.

A Year at a Building Site by Nicholas Harris (2008, 2009)—This is the story of how a school is built. The illustrations are colorful and filled with details that can be used to keep children's attention to the story over a time. Some of the workers are pictured often while others only for a short time. These details and others maintain the storyline and open opportunities for questions for and from children.

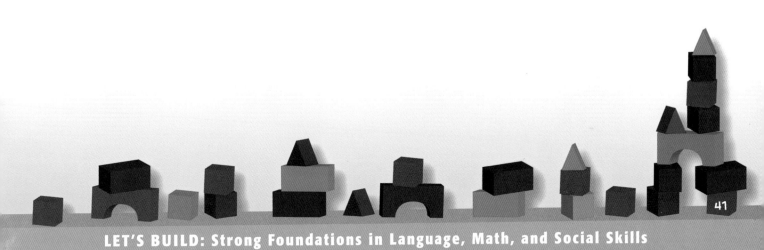

LET'S BUILD: Strong Foundations in Language, Math, and Social Skills

Assessment

To understand why didactic instruction and worksheets are not appropriate in early-childhood classrooms, it is necessary to understand the stages of play and how close observation of children's behavior and what they build and create will show evidence of their development. There are several useful scales that can be used to assess children's structured construction products. Digital cameras are a boon to any early-childhood classroom, and pictures of children's construction play products not only help with assessment and portfolio creations, but also can be used to share children's accomplishments with their families and the entire group.

One Approach to Assessment

It is important to make sure that children have ample time to play. Research and theory show that well-planned play experiences that are supported by adults who understand how young children grow and develop will provide opportunities for children to discover knowledge and develop the skills needed for later school success.

In 1933, *The Art of Block Building* by Harriett Merrill Johnson, was published for the first time. After many years of observing children building with unit blocks, Harriet Johnson presented her seven stages of block building. These seven stages hold true today and can be used to assess children's knowledge of objects in space, balance, symmetry, and their progression in representing their world symbolically.

❒ Stage 1: Carrying—basically sensorimotor

❒ Stage 2: Stacking—horizontally and vertically

❒ Stage 3: Bridging

❒ Stage 4: Enclosures

❒ Stage 5: Patterns and symmetry

❒ Stage 6: Early representational

❒ Stage 7: Later representational

Piaget (1962) considered play with blocks to be an important medium for assessing a child's ability to engage in the behaviors that will be needed in later work. Other theorists, such as Anna Freud (1968) and Erik Erikson (1963), also placed work in their continuums of development immediately after the acquisition of skills developed through play with others.

Child Development Timeline

Trust	Autonomy	Initiative	Industry
vs.	vs.	vs.	vs.
Mistrust	Shame & Doubt	Guilt	Inferiority
Sensorimotor	Pre-Operational	Concrete	
Body	Toy	Play	Work

* The Creative Center for Childhood Research and Training, Inc. (CCCRT) Concepts taken from the work of Erik Erikson, Anna Freud, and Jean Piaget

Work means that the child must be able to focus on outside rules, start and finish a project, and produce a product. These products become more and more realistic as the child matures in his or her abilities to create symbolic representations.

Block play offers teachers a window through which to observe children's work behaviors and assess the products they create. The ultimate accomplishment for a child entering kindergarten would be the creation of a structure that looks like what she says it is and that she can tell a story about how it was built and how it is used. Once the structure is finished, the child can join in play with other children and engage in a dramatic play scenario using props and sustained role-playing. Children building alone will often finish their own structure and move to another's for the dramatic play. During these experiences, children engage in structured construction play and move to dramatic play as a continuation of their structured construction play.

Two children are playing in a block area. They are in a three-year-old group and have just turned four years old. Both will move into a prekindergarten group in the fall.

CHILD #1—During the pre-scaffolding circle, the teacher reads Eric Carle's book *The Very Busy Spider* and discusses the concept of infrastructure. (The teacher shows the children how the spider connected her web to places inside the frame to create an infrastructure that would make her web strong.) After the circle, the child moves to the block area and sits down on the plywood shape that has been provided for his structure. After a few moments, he gets up and begins to choose blocks from the shelves. He places each block carefully as he begins to build. After 20 minutes of continuous focused building, he moves to the teacher, who has come by and asked questions and shown interest in the progress of the construction. "I am ready to tell you about my structure," he says. The child then begins to relate a story about how he has built a fort to keep the wild animals out and that the people live in the house in the middle. As he is telling the story, two other children move into the area, and the three of them take the zoo animals and plastic people from the prop shelf and begin a dramatic play scenario.

This structure, which used 118 blocks, features horizontal and vertical stacking, an enclosure, a pattern, and representational space with a story added, would receive a score of 7 using Johnson's scale (1933), which was described on page 42.

CHILD #2—After the same pre-scaffolding circle, he wanders about the room. The teacher encourages him to find a place to play. He had raised his hand to go to the block area while in the circle but has now lost interest. He moves around the water table picking up a turkey baster and squirting it several times. He then sits down on a small couch where books about spiders are laid out. He moves them around and continues to wander. After several more minutes, he enters the block area. A plywood shape is available for building, so he goes to the shelving and randomly picks up two different block shapes and lays them on his building shape. This unfocused, random empty-and-fill play continues for about five minutes. In between taking blocks off the shelves, he walks around the constructions of other children and is repeatedly reminded by both the children and the teacher to be careful that he doesn't step on the building shapes because someone's structure might fall down. The teacher has shown interest in him twice and finally sits down near his building shape and tries to engage him in conversation about his structure. He shrugs his shoulders and grins. No story or discussion is forthcoming. This child is not engaged and is unfocused. His is not a structure, just a pile of block pieces that receives a score of 1. This behavior tells us that this child, if left in this development stage, will have difficulty being successful in kindergarten and later school. He lacks the ability to focus on an activity and complete a project. He will need a great deal of teacher scaffolding in the coming months. Children are often hesitant to engage in activities in which they don't feel confident. It is vital that the teacher notice his lack of building interest and skill and use her knowledge to encourage his efforts. She may even need to model for this child by actually becoming a building partner, making suggestions about blocks that might be used in a construction, and providing language to describe his construction. A friendship with another child who is a builder might be encouraged so that as the child begins to become more confident, the friend can become the model and support.

45

Observation Scale for Children's Block Construction

The following scale was adapted from information in *Block Building Activities of Young Children* by Frances M. Guanella, "The structure and content of early representational play: The case of building Blocks" by Stuart Reifel, in *Young Children and Their Families,* and "Block construction: children's developmental landmarks in representation of space," an article by Stuart Reifel in Young Children. This scale is also substantiated through research conducted by the Creative Center for Childhood Research and Training, Inc. (CCCRT).

Non-Construction Use of Blocks

SCORE OF 1: NO CONSTRUCTIONS

Child investigates physical properties of blocks by engaging in noise-making, transportation, motion, experimental, and bodily contact manipulations; child engages in empty/fill play.

Linear Constructions

SCORE OF 2: VERTICAL LINEAR ARRANGEMENT

Child piles or stacks blocks.

SCORE OF 3: HORIZONTAL LINEAR ARRANGEMENT

Child places blocks side-by-side or end-to-end in a row.

LET'S BUILD: Strong Foundations in Language, Math, and Social Skills

Bi-Dimensional/Aerial Constructions

SCORE OF 4: VERTICAL AERIAL ARRANGEMENT

Child constructs adjoining piles of blocks and/or superimposes row-on-row (side-by-side stacking).

SCORE OF 5: HORIZONTAL AERIAL ARRANGEMENT

Child combines rows of blocks in a horizontal area.

Tri-Dimensional Constructions

Approximately 3 years and above

SCORE OF 6: VERTICAL SPACE

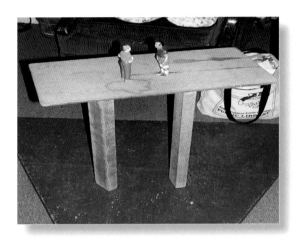 

Child places two blocks parallel and spans the space between them with a block; child forms an arch or a bridge.

SCORE OF 7: ENCLOSED HORIZONTAL SPACE

Child makes square-like shapes out of four or more blocks.

SCORE OF 8: SOLID TRI-DIMENSIONAL USE OF BLOCKS

Child makes flooring out of blocks and superimposes one or more additional layers of blocks, creating a solid tri-dimensional arrangement.

SCORE OF 9: ENCLOSED TRI-DIMENSIONAL SPACE

Child makes a roof for a horizontal enclosure, creating a tri-dimensional enclosed space.

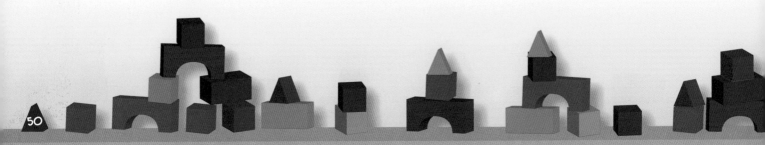

SCORE OF 10: ELABORATIONS/COMBINATIONS OF MANY CONSTRUCTION FORMS

Child uses various combinations of linear, bi-dimensional/aerial, and tri-dimensional constructions. No naming yet.

Representational Play

Approximately 3 years and above

SCORE OF 11: NAMING BEGINS

"These are airplanes."

Child names individual blocks in constructions as things. Block constructions/block shapes may or may not resemble the thing they are supposed to represent.

LET'S BUILD: Strong Foundations in Language, Math, and Social Skills

SCORE OF 12: ONE CONSTRUCTION/ONE NAME

"This is my piano."

"This is the office where my mom works."

Child uses various combinations of linear, bi-dimensional/aerial, and tri-dimensional constructions. No naming yet.

SCORE OF 13: BLOCK FORMS ARE NAMED

"These are chairs and beds for the people."

"There is a bed and a table and a TV."

Child names block forms in a construction as representing things. More than one block is used to create an object, such as a chair.

SCORE OF 14: SEPARATED OBJECTS ARE NAMED

"Mall with lights outside the entrance."

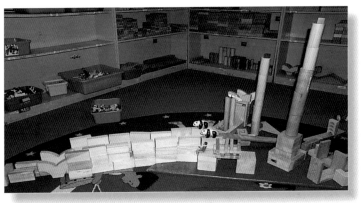

"This is a bridge with lighthouses."

Child builds constructions that include separated objects; separated objects are named.

SCORE OF 15: INTERIOR SPACE REPRESENTED

"This is the doctor's office. You go in these rooms to get a shot."

"This is the capitol. There is a zoo next door."

Child builds constructions with enclosures that represent interior space; interior space may not be totally formed.

SCORE OF 15: INTERIOR OBJECTS PLACED INTO THE EXTERIOR

"This is a hotel. The people are sleeping on the bed. There is the table where they eat."

"This is my house. The family can use the beds and other furniture."

Child builds constructions with enclosures that represent interior and exterior space; interior objects are placed outside.

SCORE OF 17: ACCURATE REPRESENTATION OF INTERIOR & EXTERIOR SPACE

"This is a big warehouse. The trucks drive in on the top floor and the people load the big boxes."

"This is a train station. You park your car outside and go inside to buy your ticket. The train is waiting."

Child builds constructions with enclosures that represent interior and exterior spaces. Inside and outside objects are separated appropriately.

SCORE OF 18: CONSTRUCTIONS BUILT TO SCALE

"These are office buildings, and an airport tower. The space between the buildings is where people can walk, but it's mostly for the planes to land, bringing people to work. There is also a little house."

Child builds constructions with block forms separated; some sense of scale in the construction.

SCORE OF 19: COMPLEX CONFIGURATIONS

Child builds a complex configuration that includes interior space, landmarks, routes, and a sense of scale.

55

Lesson Plans

The following lesson plans have broad theme topics that have been chosen because the subjects provide content that can be used for a minimum of a month. This length of time allows children's interests in the topic to be pursued and the fullness of the topic to be explored. When comprehensive themes are used in early childhood programs, state standards can be easily met as experiences are planned to support development in all domains.

The following lesson plans are written to provide a day of play experiences within a specific theme. Many of the experiences, which include painting, working with playdough, cooking, and dramatic play experiences, can be repeated throughout the month. Children need to have opportunities to repeat experiences in order to perfect their skills and knowledge. A variety of books should be read and provided for children to explore throughout the theme's duration. Only one book is chosen as the focus book of the day in these lesson plans. The focus book can and should, however, be reread numerous times.

Master teachers who have worked with young children for many years chose the themes, which have been proven through 40 years of experience to be interesting and fulfilling to both boys and girls. The lesson plans are written for 20 children and two teachers working as a team. One teacher stays near the dramatic-play and the block area to support the children's activities. The block area provides a minimum of 20 square feet of building space per child and a total block inventory of 700 pieces. The teachers in this early-childhood environment allow up to six children to play in the block area at a time. Each lesson plan uses a variety of books and offers several additional ideas for experiences other than using blocks that would support the theme.

The block area is just one area where the children play, but pieces of blocks can be used for the scaffolding circle presented for the pre-play experience. These lesson plans are written to demonstrate how blocks can become an integral part of classroom instruction. A planned demonstration or discussion along with a story and/or pictures sets the tone for the children's play and provides information that will expand the children's skill and knowledge. The book that is read does not have to be about blocks but should follow the theme topic. Each daily lesson in this book also highlights colors, as well as a shape or shapes to provide depth to the theme experience.

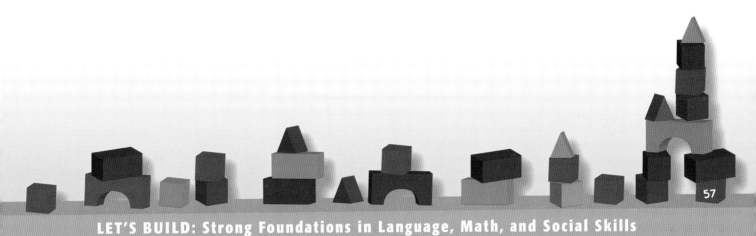

THEME I

FOCUS: Thanksgiving—-Sharing and Giving

 COLORS: • Brown • Orange • Red • Yellow

 SHAPES: Square and Cube

Half Unit

 BOOK: *Apple Farmer Annie* by Monica Wellington

 VOCABULARY: • autumn
• cornucopia
• fall
• feast
• harvest
• November
• orchard

59

Introducing the Theme Focus

❒ Fill the room with pictures of autumn scenes.

❒ Place books around the room that fit the theme.

Scaffolding the Pre-Play Experience

❒ Engage the children in a discussion about Thanksgiving, what it is, as well as the harvest and the changes of autumn.

❒ Read *Apple Farmer Annie* by Monica Wellington in the pre-play circle. Use 12 medium and tall cylinders, two double units, two quadruple units, and one floorboard to demonstrate an orchard. The floorboard is the ground; the double and quadruple units, the fencing; and the cylinders, the apple trees. Engage the children in a discussion about creating the orchard. Use rectangular-shaped blocks to show the children how they can use pieces of red, green, yellow, brown, and orange paper (represented by the blocks) to create a tree or an orchard of many trees.

❒ During this pre-scaffolding circle, introduce the play opportunities. At the close of the circle, dismiss the children in sets of one and two to play in the different centers of the classroom environment. Four children (or the number that your block/construction area accommodates) stay to play in the block area.

PLAYDOUGH RECIPE
2 cups flour
1 cup salt
4 teaspoons cream of tartar
2 tablespoons cooking oil
2 cups water
food coloring
Stir all ingredients together. Pour into skillet, stirring constantly. Cook over medium heat until completely cooked through, scraping it from the bottom, like scrambled eggs. Scoop the playdough onto a clean dry surface. Knead until cool.

Suggested Theme-Related Experiences

SENSORY/ART EXPERIENCES

❒ Make red and yellow playdough available for the children's play. Encourage them to mix the two colors. As they mix the playdough, children discover the color orange.

❒ Place water and bleach (1 tablespoon bleach in 1 gallon of cool water) into the water table. Color the water orange with red and yellow food coloring. Provide pouring, filling, and measuring equipment for the children to play and experiment with empty-and-fill play. There is space for four children to play at this table.

❒ Provide paint in the eight basic colors plus white with three different sizes of brushes (1" flat, 1/4" flat, and a small pointed brush). The children can choose construction paper in shades of red, brown, yellow, and orange, as well as manila paper (18" x 24") for their paintings.

❒ Provide construction-paper pieces and crayons in autumn colors, scissors, and glue. The children can cut and paste whatever they want, gluing the construction paper pieces and coloring on 12" x 18" pieces of manila paper.

COOKING EXPERIENCES

❒ Make this is a month full of cooking experiences, such as making apple tarts and pumpkin pies.

DRAMATIC PLAY EXPERIENCES

❒ Provide props for dramatic play scenarios related to gathering apples.

❒ Set up a fruit-and-vegetable stand in the dramatic play area

❒ Cut out a tree (or trees) from plywood. Use paper and tape or Velcro to make and hang apples and leaves on the tree (or trees). (See the photo on page 62.)

❐ Place extra pie pans, small white pieces of felt for piecrust, aprons, and cooking mitts into the kitchen of the dramatic play area.

BLOCK/CONSTRUCTION EXPERIENCE

❐ Near the block area, provide colored paper pieces (red, green, yellow, brown, and orange), markers, scissors, and tape. Tell the children that they can build anything they want to build with the blocks and that the paper and tape can be used to create trees with leaves and/or apples to decorate their structure.

HOW CHILDREN MIGHT CONTINUE
TO EXPLORE THE THEME FOCUS

After working in the block area for a while, two children might begin to build a farm and to cut paper leaves and apples and tape them onto cylinders.

Other children might build random structures after talking about these constructions with their teacher. Then, put their blocks away and leave the area to engage in other play experiences.

More children enter the block area during the hour-and-a-half play period. (This amount of time is needed for the pre-scaffolding, play, and post-scaffolding). One child may join the dramatic play now happening at the farm site and the other two children build with the blocks. **Only the child's body is involved. Toys and objects are not used. The child splashes her hands in the water in the water table or runs her hands through the sand in the sandbox.**

63

FOCUS: Our Families and Ourselves

 COLORS: Shades of Brown

 SHAPES: cCrcle and Sphere

Half Circle

 BOOK: *Houses and Homes* by Ann Morris and Ken Heyman

 VOCABULARY:
- apartment
- condominium
- duplex
- mobile home
- one-story
- symmetry
- two-story

65

Introducing the Theme Focus

❏ Fill the room with pictures of families and places where people live.

❏ Place books around the room that fit the theme.

❏ Throughout each day, such as at circle time and lunch, talk about how we are alike and different.

❏ Place hand mirrors into a basket for exploration and attach several vertical mirrors to the wall to encourage these discussions and discoveries.

❏ Ask the children to bring photos of themselves with their families and where they live to school to share. These can be used to create a bulletin board. Print the children's and their family members' names clearly in manuscript print for placement with the photographs.

❏ Take pictures of the children and their families who may have difficulty bringing in a photo as they arrive or are picked up from school.

❏ Place pictures of people of many cultures and the places where they live into a basket for the children to explore.

❏ Place books that focus on many cultures and homes in which people live where the children can explore them.

❏ Create a positive atmosphere in the classroom so everyone feels accepted.

Scaffolding the Pre-Play Experience

❏ At the beginning of the pre-play circle, read *Houses and Homes* by Ann Morris and Ken Heyman. Larger pictures of places people live can also be shared. When the book is finished, begin a discussion about where the children in the group live. As the children use different vocabulary words, such as *apartment, duplex, condominium,* and *mobile home,* write these words on a chart tablet. This promotes print awareness. (The children should not be expected to read or spell these words.) You can refer and add to this chart list as the theme progresses.

❏ Use a set of blocks to build an enclosure (use the word *enclosure* to describe the construction). Build it up a few levels and then add a floor. After beginning the second floor, begin to talk about one-story and two-story houses and what those terms mean. Ask questions such as, "Do you know anyone who lives in a two-story house?" or "Who lives in a two-story house?"

❑ During this pre-scaffolding circle, introduce the play opportunities. At the end of circle, dismiss the children in sets of one and two to play in the different centers of the classroom environment. Four children (or the number that your block/construction area accommodates) stay to play in the block area.

Suggested Theme-Related Experiences

SENSORY/ART EXPERIENCES

❑ Make pink, yellow, white, and dark brown playdough that the children made (see recipe on page 60) available for their play. The children can mix the colors of playdough to try to create their skin tone.

❒ Provide paint in skin tones along with the eight basic paint colors with small brushes for tabletop painting on 12" x 18" paper. Place approximately a tablespoon of each paint color into the cups of an egg carton. Each child has a container for washing the brushes—a pointed ½" or ¼" brush—and a piece of paper towel for drying the brush after each washing.

❒ Provide 12" x 18" manila paper pieces for use as background. Add a basket with colored pieces of construction paper, paper in skin tones, crayons in all colors and skin tones, scissors, and glue. Allow the children to cut, draw, and paste anything they want but suggest that they might make a picture of themselves, their family, or where they live. (This experience can be made available throughout the theme.)

❒ Provide construction-paper pieces and crayons in autumn colors, scissors, and glue. The children can cut and paste whatever they want, gluing the construction paper pieces and coloring on 12" x 18" pieces of manila paper.

DRAMATIC PLAY EXPERIENCES

❒ Place dress-up clothing into the dramatic play area that reflects both males and females.

❒ Set up dishpans and other materials on a table for dishwashing. On another day, plastic baby dolls can be used to provide a baby-bathing experience. Provide sponges or washcloths, and a baby dressing table can also be arranged.

❒ Plan a "family reunion" later in the week or month with a picnic in the play yard. The children can wear their dress-up clothes.

❑ Create a shoe store as an extension of the dramatic play area so children can purchase new shoes for the reunion.

BLOCK/CONSTRUCTION EXPERIENCE

❑ Make room for four children (or the appropriate number for your block area) in the block area as the children leave the pre-play circle. These children build on their plywood shapes (see page 26) for the entire playtime (1½ hours is ideal).

❑ When the structures are finished being built and the children and the teacher have discussed the construction experience, the children may move to microdramatic play props (see page 16), such as placing play people into their house constructions or acting out a scenario with the play people.

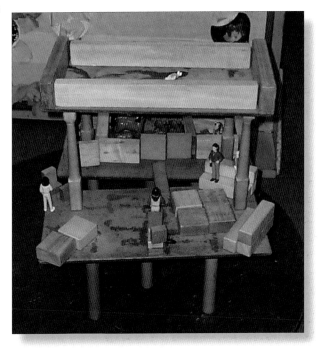

THEME 3

FOCUS: Winter and Winter Animals

 COLORS: Shades of Blue and White

 SHAPES: Rectangle

Unit

 BOOK: *The Mitten* by Jan Brett

 VOCABULARY:
- camouflage
- cold
- contraction
- expansion
- frozen
- hibernate
- ice
- snow
- symmetrical
- symmetry
- winter clothing

Introducing the Theme Focus

❑ Select books about animals in winter, winter clothing, and winter weather. Place these books around the room where children can readily review them.

❑ Hang pictures around the room that depict people, animals, and places in winter.

❑ Place on a table a basket of pairs of mittens for the children to match and a basket of single mittens and gloves near paper, markers, and crayons. Encourage the children to match the mittens (from the basket that has pairs of mittens) and to draw the missing mitten or glove (from the basket of single mittens and gloves).

❑ Discuss the concept of symmetry whenever an opportunity arises throughout the theme.

Scaffolding the Pre-Play Experience

❑ Engage the children in a discussion about the clothing they need to wear to keep warm and what animals do during the cold weather to keep warm.

❑ Read *The Mitten* at the beginning of the pre-play circle. As each animal appears in the story, write the names of the animal on a chart. At the end of the story, begin to retell the story. On a plywood board (see page 26), set out a line of unit blocks. As each animal enters the mitten, increase the space between the blocks, use the word expanded in your retelling of the story, and point to the name of the animal on the chart. At the end of the story when the mitten explodes, bring the blocks close together again. Say, "When things expand, they stretch out. When things contract, they shrink." This adds more new vocabulary words. Place several copies of *The Mitten* and a set of masks of the animals in the story in the dramatic play area where the children can explore them.

❑ During this pre-scaffolding circle, introduce the play opportunities. At the close of the circle, dismiss the children in sets of one and two to play in the different centers of the classroom environment. Four children (or the number that your block/construction area accommodates) stay to play in the block area.

Suggested Theme-Related Experiences

SENSORY/ART EXPERIENCES

- ❑ Place blue and white playdough (see recipe on page 60) onto a table for the children to mix to create shades of blue.

- ❑ Encourage the children to name the new colors they create. Write these color words on a paper where the children can display the new color playdough they created.

- ❑ Tape different shades of 18" x 24" blue construction paper across a wall for the children's easel painting. Offer nine colors of paint (red, yellow, green, blue, white, orange, purple, black, and brown) and three sizes of brushes. Encourage the children to mix the paint, including the white paint, to create new shades of colors. Provide small containers for this mixing.

- ❑ Provide a table with 12" x 18" pieces of dark and light blue construction paper and white chalk for drawing winter scenes. (Scribbles look great on the bulletin board!)

- ❑ Provide a table with 12" X 18" pieces of dark and light blue construction paper with smaller pieces of colored construction paper, crayons, scissors, and glue for creating winter scenes.

- ❑ Place water colored with blue food coloring into the water table. Add containers for emptying and filling. If the water table is set up for four children to play, provide four of each type of container and implement for emptying and filling, such as turkey basters, colanders, funnels, cups, and empty soap bottles.

- ❑ Place four 18" x 24" aluminum cookie or baking trays onto a table, two trays with white paint (tempera mixed with clear laundry detergent) and two trays with blue paint (tempera mixed with clear laundry detergent). Encourage the children to mix the paint. If they want to keep one of their creations, give them a sheet of newsprint paper (cut to the size of the trays) to make a printing of what they created (press the paper over the creation on the tray).

- ❑ Hang a sheet of butcher paper on a wall. If the children make a new and interesting shade of blue, they can make handprints in the new color on the butcher paper. Ask each child what he wants to name the color, and then write the name of the color and the child's name next to his handprints.

MICRODRAMATIC PLAY EXPERIENCES

❑ Place forest animals into dishpans or tubs. Cover the bottoms of the tubs with cornstarch and small pieces of ice. Add small fir trees (purchased at a local craft store) and a few rocks into the cornstarch. Make this available for the children's microdramatic play.

❑ When the children are outside, help them create another microdramatic play area on a tabletop with bears, laminated fish, rocks, and small fir trees. Use a piece of blue tarp to simulate water.

MACRODRAMATIC PLAY EXPERIENCES

❑ Add winter shoes, hats, mitten, gloves, scarves, and other winter clothes that are appropriate for your climate for the children to use in their dress-up play in the dramatic play area.

❑ Place a white sheet over a table to create a cave. Add soft pillows in white pillowcases to the cave. Place a few stuffed bears inside the cave to encourage the children's dramatic play. (This should not be rough-and-tumble play.) Consider adding books to encourage quiet activity.

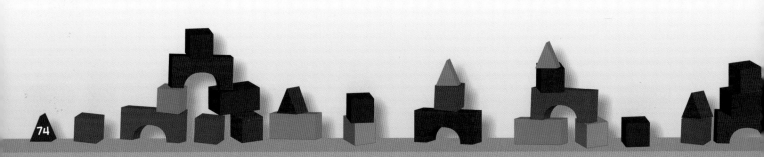

BLOCK/CONSTRUCTION EXPERIENCE
(SUPPORTING MICRODRAMATIC PLAY)

☐ Add sets of forest animals, pieces of imitation snow, and play fir trees to help move the children's constructions into dramatic play. For example, the microdramatic play props can support the children's use of their structures as places where animals hide to keep warm. The children can use the pieces of imitation snow on their buildings and on the ground in front of the buildings. The trees can be placed around in the snow.

THEME 4

FOCUS: Large Buildings Around the World

 COLORS: Shades of Green and White

 SHAPES: Triangle

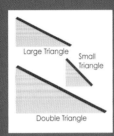

Large Triangle

Small Triangle

Double Triangle

 BOOK: *Block City* by Robert Louis Stevenson and illustrated by Daniel Kirk

 VOCABULARY:
- architect
- architecture
- castle
- cathedral
- foundation
- height
- horizontal
- names of construction vehicles
- palace
- tall
- temple
- vertical
- vessel

LET'S BUILD: Strong Foundations in Language, Math, and Social Skills

Introducing the Theme Focus

❏ Fill the room with pictures of buildings from around the world.

❏ Place books around the room that fit the theme.

❏ If possible, take the children to visit a nearby business that sells large equipment, such as front-end loaders, backhoes, excavators, and cranes. On the way, you may pass several large buildings being constructed, which leads to great discussions about jobs, tools, equipment, and other related subjects.

❏ Create a word list of new vocabulary terms after returning from the trip to the nearby business.

❏ Place books about construction around the classroom environment, along with pictures of great constructions around the world, such as the Eiffel Tower in Paris, the great Pyramid in Egypt, the Coliseum in Rome, and the Taj Mahal in India.

Scaffolding the Pre-Play Experience

❏ During the pre-play circle, read to the children "Block City," a famous poem written by Robert Louis Stevenson and reprinted on page 79. Read the poem first to help the children develop listening skills and the ability to create pictures in their imagination, and then read the poem a second time, stopping to ask questions such as, "Where do you think this child is?" or "Why is he inside?"

❏ Display the poem on chart paper and revisit it throughout the theme.

❏ Hang pictures of the buildings mentioned in the poem (castles, palaces, temples, and docks) throughout the classroom.

❏ Add new words from the poem to the vocabulary list.

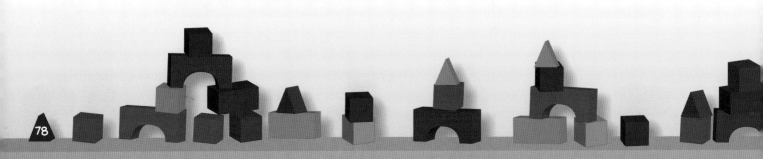

BLOCK CITY by Robert Louis Stevenson

What are you able to build with your blocks?
Castles and palaces, temples and docks.
Rain may keep raining, and others go roam,
But I can be happy and building at home.

Let the sofa be mountains, the carpet be sea,
There I'll establish a city for me:
A kirk and a mill and a palace beside,
And a harbor as well where my vessels may ride.

Great is the palace with pillar and wall,
A sort of a tower on top of it all,
And steps coming down in an orderly way
To where my toy vessels lie safe in the bay.

This one is sailing and that one is moored:
Hark to the song of the sailors on board!
And see on the steps of my palace the kings
Coming and going with presents and things!

❑ During this pre-scaffolding circle, introduce the play opportunities. At the end of the circle, dismiss the children in sets of one and two to play in the different centers of the classroom environment. Four children (or the number that your block/construction area accommodates) stay to play in the block area.

79

Suggested Theme-Related Experiences

SENSORY/ART EXPERIENCES

- ❑ Place the homemade green and white playdough (see page 60) onto a table for the children to mix and create new shades of green. Ask the children to name the new colors they create, and then write these words on chart paper where the new color could be displayed.

- ❑ Place 12" x 18" pieces of manila paper onto a table with markers for drawing buildings. (Let the children draw whatever they want. The building drawing is just a suggestion.)

- ❑ Place onto a table scissors, crayons, different sizes of triangle templates, and pieces of different colors of paper for cutting triangles. Provide sheets of 12" x 18" manila paper for the children to paste their triangles onto.

- ❑ Place four 18" x 24" aluminum cookie or baking trays onto a table, two trays with white paint (tempera mixed with clear laundry detergent) and two trays with green paint (tempera mixed with clear laundry detergent). Encourage the children to mix the paint. If they make a creation that they want to keep, give them a sheet of newsprint paper (cut to the size of the trays) to make a printing of what they created (press the paper over the representation on the tray).

- ❑ Hang a sheet of butcher paper on the wall. If the children make a new and interesting shade of green, they can make handprints in the new color on the butcher paper. Ask the child what she wants to name the color, and then write the name of the color and the child's name next to her handprints.

- ❑ Provide green construction paper and manila paper for easel painting (18" x 24" for both). Allow the children to choose the color of paper they want to use and whether to place the paper horizontally or vertically onto the painting board (chalkboard where four children can comfortably paint side by side works well for this).

- ❑ Make available crayons, markers, and paper (12" x 18" manila) at a table for drawing buildings and floor plans. (Ask the children's parents or a local architect if they have architectural drawings that the children may use. If so, tape some of these to the wall nearest the table.)

DRAMATIC PLAY EXPERIENCES

❏ Support the children's ideas, such as building a pyramid out of large pieces of cardboard connected with wide tape. The pyramid could have a door so the children can go inside. The pyramid can also be painted with wide brushes and brown and yellow paints.

❏ Another idea is to create a castle wall out of cardboard and place it at the entrance to the indoor or outdoor dramatic play area. You (or another adult) can draw stone shapes that the children can paint with black and gray shades of tempera paint. Make costumes available inside the dramatic-play area to support king-and-queen play for both girls and boys. Make pieces of lacy and shiny fabrics available to tie into capes, veils, and other embellishments to the costumes.

❏ Cut pieces of poster board into crown shapes and provide shiny pieces of paper, glue, and scissors on a table outside the dramatic play area for the children to make crowns. Consider purchasing special plastic stone shapes at a local craft store for children to use to decorate their crowns.

BLOCK/CONSTRUCTION EXPERIENCES

❏ Place paper, popsicle sticks of different widths and colors, scissors, and glue onto a table so the children can create three-dimensional constructions.

❏ Provide a floor space or tabletop for play with Legos or other structured construction materials.

❏ Place construction hats near the block area to support the construction theme. Be sure pictures of large buildings are available for the children to explore.

❑ In the accompanying photo, you can see a construction created by two children working together to build a cathedral. When they finished their construction, they continued their play using micro-dramatic play props.

THEME 5

FOCUS: Birds

 COLORS: Red and Blue

 SHAPES: Circles

Half Circle

 BOOK: *Owl Babies* by Martin Waddell

 VOCABULARY:
- beak
- claws
- eggs
- feathers
- flightless
- hover
- nests
- nocturnal
- predators
- talons
- wings

Introducing the Theme Focus

❑ Engage the children in a discussion about birds that fly and the ones that do not. All birds have feathers and lay eggs, but all birds do not fly or build nests. If you live where there are hummingbirds, consider hanging two hummingbird feeders with sugar water outside a window (one part dissolved sugar to four parts water), or hang several seed-filled birdfeeders from the trees on the playground and keep a birdbath clean and filled with fresh water.

❑ Select books about birds and place these books around the classroom onto shelves and into baskets.

❑ Add reference books about birds that will help answer questions that the children have about some of the birds, such as ostriches, emperor penguins, and condors (vulture).

❑ Display pictures of birds, nests, and eggs for the children to inspect.

❑ Add to the focus by having the children make pretend binoculars from paper towel rolls and going on several bird-watching walks. Use a bird book to identify the birds that you see on your bird-watching walks or simply outside your window.

Scaffolding the Pre-Play Experience

❑ Read *Owl Babies* to the children in the pre-play circle. Tell the children that owls are nocturnal and that they catch small animals for food with their strong beaks and talons. Engage the children in a discussion after reading of the book. Start a vocabulary list.

❑ Use the block area to lay out a string the length of a condor's wingspan (approximately 10'). Suggest that the children use difference kinds and sizes of blocks to measure the wingspan (nonstandard measuring).

❑ Make a graph on a large piece of white paper depicting the different block shapes and the number needed to equal the length of the condor wingspan. This project can take several days to complete. The children can also lie down in the middle of the string to see how much larger the wingspan is than their arm reach.

❑ During this pre-scaffolding circle, introduce the play opportunities. At the end of the circle, dismiss the children in sets of one and two to play in the different centers of the classroom environment. Four children (or the number that your block/construction area accommodates) stay to play in the block area.

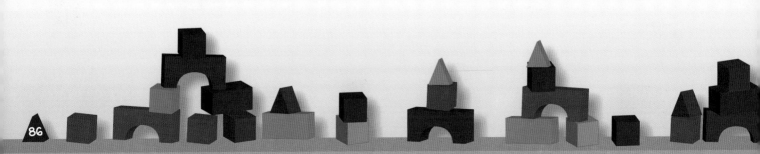

Suggested Theme-Related Experiences

SENSORY/ART EXPERIENCES

❑ Have art paper (18" x 24") available for easel painting. Allow the children to choose whether their paper is placed horizontally or vertically onto the painting board (chalkboard where children can comfortably paint side by side). Provide paint in the eight basic colors plus white and three sizes of brushes. Use small, recycled containers for the children to mix new colors.

❑ Set out homemade red and blue playdough (see recipe on page 60) so that mixing and creating purple is possible.

❑ Place four 18" x 24" aluminum cookie or baking trays onto a table, two trays with red paint (tempera mixed with clear laundry detergent) and two trays with blue paint (tempera mixed with clear laundry detergent). Encourage the children to mix the paint. If they make a creation that they want to keep, give them a sheet of newsprint paper (cut to the size of the trays) to make a printing (press the paper over the creation in the tray).

- Hang a sheet of butcher paper onto the wall. If the children make a new and interesting shade of purple, they can make handprints in the new color on the butcher paper. Ask the child what she wants to name the color, and then write the name of the color and the child's name next to her handprints.

- Offer 12" x 18" art paper, small brushes, glue, and small amounts of tempera paint in egg cartons. Save eggshells, soak them in a bleach solution, and let them dry. The children can crumble the eggshells, and glue them onto the paper to create eggshell pictures. The children can paint the eggshells on their paper with tempera paint to add color.

- Provide a table with 12" x 18" pieces of manila paper, scissors, crayons or markers, pieces of colored construction paper, and glue so that the children can cut and create their on products.

SENSORY/SOUND EXPERIENCE

- During the children's playtime, softly play a tape with birdcalls.

COOKING EXPERIENCES

- Make birdseed cornbread to feed the birds (recipe follows) and a pan of regular cornbread with frozen kernel corn baked in it for snack time. Serve the children's cornbread with honey and milk, and hang pieces of the birdseed cornbread from the trees. The children can take home any remaining pieces of the birdseed cornbread to put in their own yards.

- Print the recipe clearly on a chart so that the children can "read" the recipe and help count the ingredients. Send a copy of the recipe home with the children so they can make this cornbread with their families for the birds in their yard.

- Note: The following recipe makes enough for 20 children to each have a piece to take home. You may need to change the recipe to meet the needs of your class.

BIRDSEED CORNBREAD RECIPE

Ingredients:

cooking spray

2 cups all-purpose flour, sifted

2 cups yellow cornmeal

1 cup white sugar

2 1/2 teaspoons salt

7 teaspoons baking powder

2 eggs

2 cups milk

2/3 cup vegetable oil

2 cups mixed wild birdseed (To make edible cornbread, replace the birdseed with corn kernels.)

Equipment:

2 bowls—one to sift the flour into and one large enough to mix the ingredients

large spoons for stirring

sifter

measuring spoons

measuring cups for dry ingredients

measuring cup for wet ingredients

1" deep x 12" wide x 18" long sheet-cake pan

cooling rack

plastic bags

DIRECTIONS

Preheat oven to 400 degrees F.

Coat with cooking spray or lightly grease the sheet-cake pan.

Allow the children to take turns sifting the flour into a large bowl. The exact amount can be measured when the sifting process is completed.

Allow the children to compare the texture, smell, and taste of the sugar, corn meal, and flour. Encourage the use of descriptive words such as grainy, smooth, sweet, and powdery. Repeat the words that the children use to describe the three ingredients so all the children can hear the words. The flour holds the other ingredients together. The flour and the cornmeal are the "bones" of the cornbread, and the sugar makes it taste sweet.

When the eggs are added, be sure to discuss the possibility of salmonella on the eggs, and have the children who handle the eggs wash their hands again. (Salmonella is bacteria, a microscopic organism, found on some foods. It can make us very ill if we do not handle the food carefully. Eggshells can have salmonella bacteria on them.)

In a large bowl, combine flour, cornmeal, sugar, salt, and baking powder. Stir in egg, milk and vegetable oil until well combined. Add the birdseed and stir until smooth. Be sure to let the children compare the sizes, colors, and other characteristics of the birdseed.

Pour the batter into prepared pan. You now have a thick liquid mixture. You can discuss the thickness (viscosity) of the mixture with the children. Compare it to the milk. When the batter is fully cooked, the liquid will have evaporated and the cornbread will become a solid.

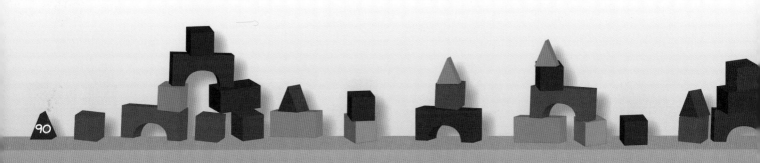

Directions cont.

Bake in a preheated oven for 20 to 25 minutes or until a toothpick inserted into the center of the cornbread comes out clean. Let the cornbread cool in the pan and then slice it into pieces. Make enough pieces so there are some to put outside to feed the birds and so each child can take a piece home. Place each piece into a plastic bag for the children to take home to feed the birds.

Remake this same recipe without the birdseed. Kernel corn can be added to make a delicious snack for the children to eat. Cornbread without the birdseed can be baked in advance so that the children can taste it. A little butter, syrup, or honey will make this a real treat.

DRAMATIC PLAY EXPERIENCE

❑ Place the bottom of several large boxes near the dramatic play area. Provide small sticks, pieces of cotton, hay, and small pieces of cloth and yarn for the children to use to create bird nests. Add bird puppets for the children to use in the nests and bird books for reference.

THEME 6

FOCUS: Insects and Spiders

 COLORS: Shades of Green

 SHAPES: Hexagon

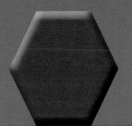 

 BOOK: *The Very Busy Spider* by Eric Carle

 VOCABULARY:
- abdomen
- aquarium
- caterpillar
- chrysalis
- cocoon
- larva
- pupa
- symmetrical
- symmetry
- terrarium
- thorax
- web

LET'S BUILD: Strong Foundations in Language, Math, and Social Skills

Introducing the Theme Focus

☐ Engage the children in a discussion about insects and spiders, how they are alike and how they are different. Many insects are helpful and contribute to our well-being, such as ladybugs and house spiders that eat biting insects.

☐ Consider growing parsley, fennel, and dill in garden boxes to attract butterflies.

☐ *If possible, watch butterfly caterpillars hatch from their eggs and eat and eat until they create a chrysalis and then emerge as butterflies.

☐ Hang pictures of insects and spiders in the room.

☐ Fill the classroom with fiction and nonfiction books of insects and spiders.

☐ ***Note from the author:*** One year, a large brown house spider lived in the corner of the block area, and the children watched her as she made her web and then grew her egg sac. A large number of baby spiders hatched out of the sac, much to everyone's delight.

Scaffolding the Pre-Play Experience

- ☐ Start the pre-play circle with a reading of *The Very Busy Spider*. After discussing the story, take six double units from the block shelf and arrange the blocks into a hexagon shape. Count the sides of the shape with the children and talk about how hexa means "six." If possible, show the children a poster with buildings that have the hexagon shape in their architecture as well as pictures of objects that use the hexagon shape.

- ☐ Ask the children to look around the classroom for objects that have the hexagon shape, such as parquetry pieces and geometric shapes that could be used on a light table.

- ☐ Suggest that the children try to use the hexagon shape in the buildings that they construct in the block area. Display a photo of buildings that use hexagons where the children who are in the block area can easily see the photo. Place pictures of windows and other objects using the hexagon shape onto a shelf.

- ☐ **Note:** Display the photos that are part of this book, or use an Internet search engine to find photos of buildings that use a hexagon shape as part of their design.

- ☐ During this pre-scaffolding circle (which takes place in the open space of the block area), introduce the play opportunities. At the close of the circle, dismiss the children in sets of one and two to play in the different centers of the classroom environment. Four children (or the number that your block/construction area accommodates) stay to play in the block area.

Suggested Theme-Related Experiences

SENSORY/ART EXPERIENCES

- ☐ Place two 18" x 24" aluminum cookie or baking trays onto a table, one with white tempera paint with clear liquid detergent and one with green tempera with clear liquid detergent on the other. Encourage the children to mix the colors and create shades of green that they use to make handprints on a piece of white paper taped to a nearby tabletop. Ask the children the names of their new shades and write the names of the colors and the children's names on the paper.

- ☐ Cut large hexagon shapes from butcher paper and tape them to the chalkboard, creating easel painting spaces. Offer the eight basic colors plus white of tempera paint and three different sizes of brushes in each paint container.

- Provide the following art materials and tools to make a spider:

    - brown and black construction paper

    - scissors and templates in the shape of a large and small circle, an oval, and a hexagon for drawing shapes

    - glue, chalk, buttons, and googly eyes

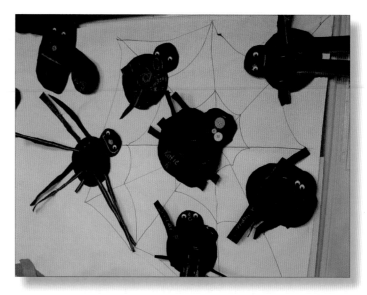

- Offer supervision and guidance to the children as they create spiders with the materials. Hang the finished spiders onto a web drawn on a bulletin board. Let the children cut spider legs and body parts. Cardboard geometric-shape templates can be used to help the children successfully create the needed body parts. They should be allowed to draw around the templates and cut out the shapes themselves.

- Color water green with food coloring and bleach (1 tablespoon bleach to 1 gallon cool water) and add to the water table. Offer pouring, filling, and measuring equipment for the children's play and experimentation.

- Offer 12" x 18" pieces art paper, shades of green crayons and markers in a basket, different shades of construction paper, and scissors. Place templates of different hexagon sizes onto the table for tracing. The children can draw hexagon shapes or glue the shapes onto paper.

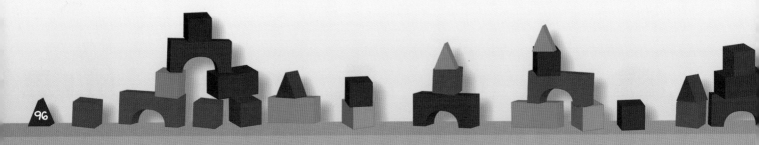

- Purchase a bag of small plastic spiders (one for each child). Set up a table with black construction paper (12" x 18"), white yarn cut into long and short pieces, and liquid glue. Provide pictures of spider webs for the children to examine and/or take an early morning walk around the playground looking for spider webs in the trees and on the ground. Let the children paint the glue on the black paper and then swirl the yarn into web shapes. When their web is complete, they can place their spider onto the web. Place a drop of hot glue (a teacher-only step) where the children choose to secure the spider to the web.

- **Note from the author:** One year, a child brought his father's pet tarantula to share. The spider was kept safely in a secure terrarium, and the children watched it with magnifying glasses.

DRAMATIC PLAY EXPERIENCES

- Create ladybug and butterfly costumes for the dramatic play area. Place several small open cardboard boxes onto the floor. Help the children make brown chrysalises with cutouts for faces out of the cardboard and butterfly wings out of poster board. Cut slits into the butterfly wings where hands can fit through. Reinforce the slits with strong tape. The children will enjoy reenacting the life cycle of the butterfly.

- Draw a large web with chalk or make one out of white rope. Place the web onto an open floor area in the classroom or outside on a cement area or the ground. Let children pretend to be spiders taking turns as they walk around on the web using their hands and feet.

MANIPULATIVES EXPERIENCE

- Offer a large floor puzzle depicting insects and two parquetry sets at a table.

THEME 7

FOCUS: The Ocean and Ocean Life

 COLORS: Shades of Blue

 **SHAPES:** Octagon

 BOOK: *The Little Red Lighthouse and the Great Gray Bridge* **by Hildegard Swift**

 VOCABULARY: • names of common shells, such as: *scallop, conch, whelk,* and so on; names of ocean animals, such as *whales, shrimp, octopi, coral, seals, squid, sharks,* and so on

• **octagon**

Introducing the Theme Focus

❐ Engage the children in a discussion about the ocean and the animals that live in the ocean.

❐ Hang pictures around the room of animals that live in the oceans.

❐ Fill the classroom with fiction and nonfiction books about oceans and the animals that live in the ocean.

Scaffolding the Pre-Play Experience

❐ Engage the children in a discussion about the animals that live in the oceans. Start a chart list of vocabulary words for the theme.

❐ Read *The Little Red Lighthouse and the Great Gray Bridge* by Hildegard Swift. You can read this wonderful book about the little red lighthouse several times throughout this theme and then discuss with the children how the little lighthouse continued to help even though the huge bridge towered over it. The concept of **big and little** is a focus of this story. Use several blocks to demonstrate the concept of bridging. Show the children pictures of different kinds of bridges.

❐ During this pre-scaffolding circle, which takes place in the open space of the block area, introduce the play opportunities. At the close of the circle, dismiss the children in sets of one and two to play in the different centers of the classroom environment. Four children (or the number that your block/construction area accommodates) stay to play in the block area

Suggested Theme-Related Experiences

SENSORY/ART EXPERIENCES

❐ Place colored chalk and 12" x 18" construction paper in two shades of blue onto a table for the children to make underwater ocean pictures.

❐ Place blue and white playdough onto a table. Encourage the children to create new shades of blue by mixing the two colors of playdough. When the children create new colors, ask them the names of the colors and write the names of the new colors on a chart.

❐ Have shades of blue construction or manila paper (18" x 24") available for easel painting. Allow the children to choose whether their paper is placed horizontally or vertically onto the painting board (chalkboard where children can comfortably paint side by side). Provide paint in the eight basic colors plus white and three sizes of brushes. Use small, recycled containers for the children to mix new colors.

MICRODRAMATIC PLAY EXPERIENCE

☐ Create a microdramatic play area in a water table by placing approximately 2" of white sand on the bottom of the water table and then putting shells on top of the sand. Add water colored with blue food coloring to the water table and then float pieces of different shades of green yarn on the top of the water for seaweed. Place sea animals into a basket beside the water table to support the children's play.

DRAMATIC PLAY EXPERIENCES

❑ Extend the dramatic play area to include a seafood restaurant. Some children can "cook" in the kitchen while others pretend to be customers sitting at small tables. Use menus donated by a local restaurant. Use dress-up clothing for the children to prepare for their night out at the restaurant. In your pre-play circle, discuss seafood restaurants, what you can order and what the roles are in the restaurant. Make a chart that lists that could be ordered, such as shrimp, crab, fish, grits, and salad and the roles in a restaurant, such as waiters, waitress, host, hostess, cooks, chefs, and customers.

❑ Children love dressing up and taking on the various roles a restaurant scenario offers. You can set up this dramatic play opportunity inside or outside.

PUPPET PLAY EXPERIENCE

❑ Turn a rectangular table onto its side to create a puppet stage. Place chairs in front of the stage for the audience and a basket with ocean life puppets behind the stage.

BOOK EXPERIENCE

❑ Place books about sea life throughout the room. Create a soft, cozy area in one corner of the room near the dramatic play area by arranging beach towels and blow-up pillows on the floor. Place two child-sized lounge chairs near the beach towels, and use a tape player or digital music device to play ocean sounds.

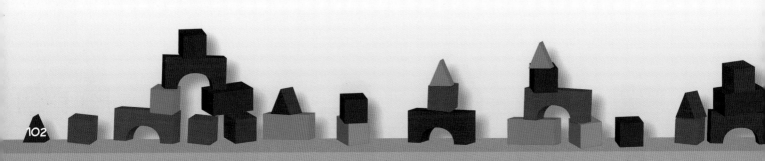

MATH/SORTING EXPERIENCES

❏ Provide a box of shells of different kinds and sizes on a table for sorting and classifying. Offer magnifying glasses for close observation.

❏ Place a tub of plastic sea creatures onto the floor next to a graphing mat. Make available two clipboards with pencils for writing numerals.

MANIPULATIVES EXPERIENCE

❏ Provide a large ocean floor puzzle.

BLOCK/CONSTRUCTION EXPERIENCES

❏ Support the building of an "ocean liner" using large hollow blocks for children to play inside.

❏ Share books about and pictures of ocean liners.

❏ Place pictures of bridges into the block area for the children to look at as well as several copies of The Little Red Light House and the Great Gray Bridge. Encourage the building of boats, ships, lighthouses, and bridges.

Note from the author: During this topic, a group of children created a large bridge with two lighthouses beside it. Two panda bears were placed at the beginning of the bridge to guard it.

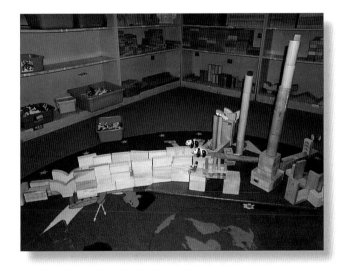

LET'S BUILD: Strong Foundations in Language, Math, and Social Skills

THEME 8

FOCUS: Amphibians and Reptiles

 COLORS: Shades of Green and Brown

 SHAPES: Rectangle

Unit   Double Unit

 BOOK: *A Color of His Own* by Leo Lionni

 VOCABULARY:
- alligators
- crocodiles
- eggs
- elongated
- frogs
- lizards
- nonvenomous
- reptilian
- salamanders
- scales
- scaly
- slimy
- slithering
- snakes
- toads
- venomous

LET'S BUILD: Strong Foundations in Language, Math, and Social Skills

Introducing the Theme Focus

❑ Display books about reptiles and amphibians, both fiction and nonfiction, on shelves for easy access by the children.

❑ Hang around the room pictures of amphibians and reptiles.

❑ Fill the classroom with fiction and nonfiction books about oceans and the animals that live in the ocean.

Scaffolding the Pre-Play Experience

This kind of experience and information builds a foundation for children's future success and learning. Children can retrieve this information when needed to understand concepts being discussed.

❑ Engage the children in a discussion about amphibians and reptiles.

❑ Start a list of amphibians and one of reptiles on chart paper, as you read books and as the children bring pictures and books from home about these animals.

❑ Young children love learning about these animals, and there are many books and pictures available to enrich this topic. Read *A Color of His Own* by Leo Lionni. This story is about a little lizard that doesn't like his color. It is a great story about diversity as well as a reptile. At the end of the story, talk about the differences between amphibians and reptiles.

　○ Reptiles have scales, and amphibians have smooth skin.

　○ They are both cold-blooded (can't keep themselves warm).

　○ Amphibians live some part of their lives in water.

　○ Reptiles have toenails, and amphibians do not.

　○ Reptiles look like their parents at birth, and amphibians do not.

　○ Reptiles lay hard-shelled eggs, and amphibian eggs are soft and must be laid in water (children love this kind of information).

❑ After the pre-play circle, dismiss the children to the areas in the classroom where they want to play.

Note from the author: A child worked for more than thirty minutes to create the alligator construction in this photo. He was very proud of his construction. The teacher invited the children in the room to come and look. The child told the children that it was a mother alligator, and she was protecting her baby.

Suggested Theme-Related Experiences

SENSORY/ART EXPERIENCES

❑ Place four 18" x 24" cookie trays onto a tabletop, two of the trays with orange tempera paint (with clear liquid laundry detergent) and two with purple tempera paint (with clear liquid laundry detergent). When the children mix the colors, they create shades of brown. Tape a large piece of white butcher paper onto a nearby wall so the children can make handprints of their new colors on the paper. Write the names of the colors the children created and the children's names next to the handprints.

❑ Make available a table with crayons, markers, and 12" x 18" art paper for drawing.

❑ Place orange and purple playdough (see recipe on page 60) onto a table for creating amphibians and reptiles and mixing new shades of brown.

❐ Provide paint in eight colors plus white and sheets of 18" x 24" manila art paper, and shades of brown and green construction paper. Let the children choose whether they want their paper placed horizontally or vertically onto the painting board. Arrange this experience at the chalkboard so the children can paint side by side.

DRAMATIC PLAY EXPERIENCES

❐ Provide ample clothing and other props to support the play of the children in the dramatic play area. Consider creating a pet store specializing in reptiles and amphibians. Add small boxes (not much larger than a shoebox) for the children to make habitats using plastic plants and vines gathered at garage sales and craft stores. Place small plastic snakes, frogs, lizards, and other animals into baskets on the worktable. Add crayons, markers, green, brown, and yellow construction paper pieces, scissors, and glue.

❐ Cut down a cardboard box so that only a 3" edge remains. Provide rocks, plastic greenery, and sticks along with small plastic reptiles and amphibians for microdramatic play.

Note from the author: During this topic, one child brought in his pet African Dwarf frogs in an aquarium. Magnifying glasses and two chairs were placed near the tank so the children could observe them closely.

MICRODRAMATIC PLAY EXPERIENCE

❏ Purchase a plastic cement-mixing tub (approximate 26" x 20") and fill it with dirt. Dig the dirt out of one end, and place a large black garbage bag into this space as a liner. Pour water into the liner. Float a few small sticks with ferns on the water, and place some non-toxic greenery into the dirt, along with some smooth rocks. Place plastic alligators, frogs, and a few snakes into the tub. This makes a wonderful microdramatic play area.

SOFT CONSTRUCTION AND READING EXPERIENCE

❏ Help the children make a large boa constrictor by sewing different colored pieces of cloth together into a long cylinder. Make the boa approximately a foot in diameter and then stuff it with stuffing. Place a quilt on the floor and then create a square shape made from one height of hollow blocks. Add the boa, small pillows,

and books about amphibians into the square shape created by the blocks. This makes a soft reading area where the children can snuggle with the boa. Of course, prepare for hearing the song "I'm Being Swallowed by a Boa Constrictor" numerous times.

MANIPULATIVES EXPERIENCE

❏ Make available a floor puzzle depicting rain-forest animals, (many amphibians and reptiles are rain-forest animals) in a low-traffic area on a carpet. Helping the children to count the different animals once the puzzle is completed can extend this experience. For example, ask, "How many butterflies are in this puzzle?" If paper, pencil, and clipboard are available, a list can be made using roughly drawn sketches of the animals, the word that labels (names) each animal, and the number of each animal in the puzzle. A graph could also be created from this experience. Answering questions such as which animal appears the most (the largest set of animals), and which animal appears the least (the smallest set of animals), adds a mathematical element to the experience.

THEME 9

FOCUS: Ways to Travel—Vehicles, Planes, and Trains

 COLORS: Red, Yellow, and Green

 SHAPES: Octagon (Shape of a Stop Sign)

 BOOK: *Trains* by Gail Gibbons

 VOCABULARY:
- cargo planes
- charter buses
- city buses
- freight trains
- jet planes
- passenger trains
- pickup trucks
- school buses
- semitrailer trucks

111

Introducing the Theme Focus

- ❐ Engage children in a discussion about where they have traveled and the kinds of transportation they have used to get to different places.

- ❐ Sing train songs such as the "Little Red Caboose" and "Down by the Station."

- ❐ Display traffic signs around the room and talk about the signs.

- ❐ Discuss the colors of traffic lights—red, green, and yellow.

- ❐ Display the room with pictures of different types of transportation.

- ❐ Place books around the room that fit the theme.

- ❐ **Note from the author:** If possible, arrange for different vehicles to visit your school. At different times, the author has had a bus, a semitrailer, an emergency truck, and a fire truck visit the school.

Scaffolding the Pre-Play Experience

- ❐ Read *Trains* by Gail Gibbons. This simple book depicts different kinds of trains and the work that they do. Make a chart that lists all the different kinds of transportation that the children have taken.

- ❐ When the circle is over, the children should choose their play experiences in small groups or individually. This provides some control about what children choose and makes the transition orderly. Those who want to play in the block area remain because circle time takes place in the large, open space of the block area.

Note from the author: During this topic, one boy built the passenger plane he had ridden in to visit his grandmother. Another child had ridden on a train all the way to Washington, DC. She worked for more than 40 minutes to reproduce the huge train station, and a third child created a tollbooth where cars stopped and paid.

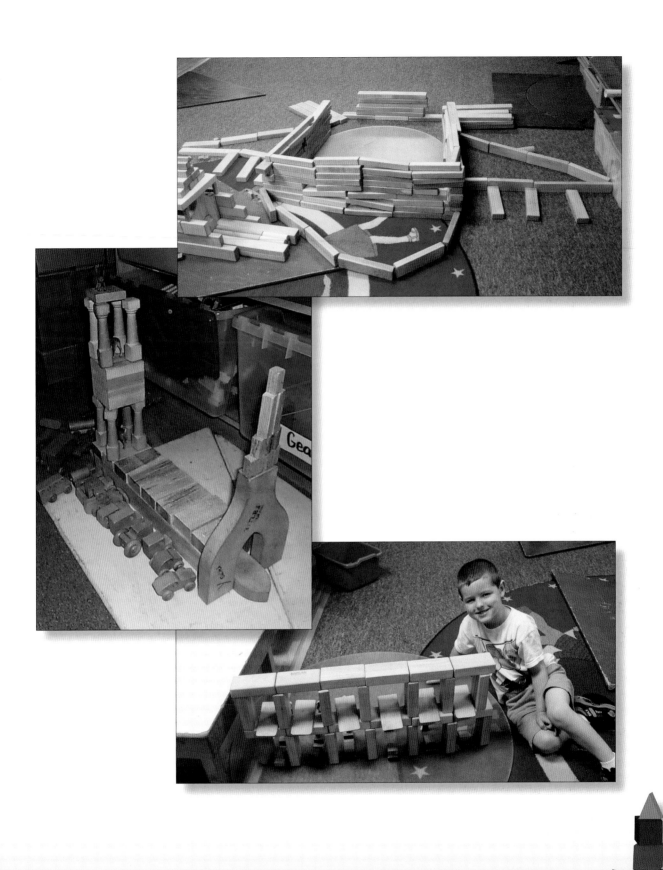

113

Suggested Theme-Related Experiences

SENSORY/ART EXPERIENCES

❒ Make available an easel area on the chalkboard with 18" x 24" art paper, eight colors of tempera paint, and three sizes of paintbrushes per container of paint. The children can paint side-by-side.

❒ Arrange several large octagon templates, scissors, markers, pieces of thin white poster board, and crayons on a table for the children to use to make traffic signs. Engage the children to make their own signs, share them with the other children in a post-play circle, and then hang the signs around the room.

DRAMATIC PLAY EXPERIENCES

❒ Use a large cardboard box (with one side removed) to create a bus. Place chairs inside the box along with a seat for the driver. The children can sell bus tickets at a desk in the dramatic play area, and they can pack suitcases with playhouse clothing, then dress and board the bus for their trips.

❒ Reminder: Keep the general playhouse open for the children's play.

LITERACY EXPERIENCES

❒ Place different traffic signs and fiction and nonfiction books about ways to travel around the room.

❒ Laminate pictures of methods of transportation and place them onto metal rings for the children to explore.

❒ Make available paper, pointed markers, crayons, and pencils for the children to make their own books about "Ways to Travel." The children can create their own pictures and dictate what they want written on their pages. You either write their dictation or write individual words onto cards for the children to copy. The children work on their book over the entire theme period. When they are finished, they make a cover from construction paper. Each child's book will be unique.

❒ Make a library corner with child-sized chairs, pillows, and a couch. Place fiction and nonfiction books about transportation onto a small nearby shelf and into a basket.

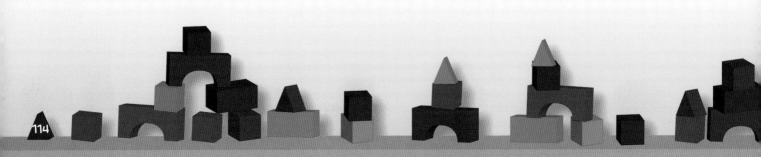

MANIPULATIVES EXPERIENCES

❏ Provide a large set of Legos with vehicles in a low-traffic area of the floor. Place the tub of Legos onto a plywood geometric shape (see page 26) to help the children know where to keep their play.

❏ Make available containers of train track, buildings, engines, and cars in another low-traffic area of the room.

❏ Arrange puzzles depicting vehicles, trains, and planes onto a table.

❏ Place a container of plastic six different plastic vehicles in six different colors onto the floor next to a vinyl-graphing mat for the children to use to classify the vehicles. Add two clipboards with pencils for counting sets and writing numerals.

THEME 10

FOCUS: Wild Animals

 COLORS: Yellow, Orange, Black, and Brown

 SHAPES: Half Circles and Domes

Half Circle   Quarter Circle

 BOOK: *Who Is the Beast?* by Keith Barker

 VOCABULARY:
- apes
- camouflaged
- endangered
- jungle
- monkeys
- plains
- protected
- rain forest
- wild animal names
- zoo

LET'S BUILD: Strong Foundations in Language, Math, and Social Skills

Introducing the Theme Focus

- ❐ Engage the children in a discussion about wild animals.

- ❐ Place into the block area a poster showing buildings with half circles and domes in their architecture.

- ❐ Learn many interesting facts about wild animals, readily available in nonfiction books and on the Internet.

- ❐ Hang pictures of wild animals in the room.

- ❐ Place fiction and nonfiction books about wild animals around the room.

Scaffolding the Pre-Play Experience

- ❐ Read *Who Is The Beast?* by Keith Barker. The illustrations in this book are filled with beautiful patterns, and the use of color is exotic. This book provides a great opportunity to discuss animals in the rain forest as well as the topic of diversity. All the animals have eyes and tails for example.

- ❐ Point out the pictures of buildings with half circles and domes in their architecture.

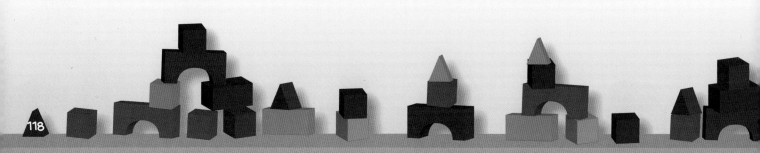

- ❏ Show the children the half-circle block shapes and domes.

- ❏ When the circle is over, the children decide where they are going to play. Those who want to play in the block area remain because circle time takes place in the large, open space of the block area.

Note from the author: Wild-animal families were added to the props in the block area to support the new play theme. This photo depicts a zoo that was created by several children, who continued to play with the new animal-family props throughout most of the playtime.

Suggested Theme-Related Experiences

SENSORY/ART EXPERIENCES

- ❏ Set up an easel painting area on the chalkboard with 18" x 24" art paper, eight colors of tempera paint, and paintbrushes in three sizes in each container. The children can paint side-by-side. Encourage the children to choose whether to hang their paper horizontally or vertically for painting.

- ❏ Provide large, lightweight paper plates, orange and black construction paper, wiggly eyes, markers, scissors, yarn for tying, and glue for the children to use to make tiger masks. Hang pictures of tigers onto the shelf or onto the wall behind the art table.

DRAMATIC PLAY EXPERIENCES

❒ Make a safari truck from chairs and a large flat piece of cardboard attached to one side. The children can dress in the playhouse and then ride on the pretend safari truck looking for wild animals through binoculars they make from cut paper towels rolls.

Note from the author: During this topic, we read *Rumble in the Jungle* by Giles Andreae and then set up a jungle scene with plywood trees with large paper palm leaves attached, large piece of imitation grass, and a piece of blue tarp to create a pool. With the addition of the tiger masks being made in the art area, this became a place to reenact jungle scenarios. The scene was later moved to the playground for continued play. (Remember tigers live in India and Asia, not in Africa. Lions live in Africa.)

LITERACY EXPERIENCES

❒ Select fiction and nonfiction books about wild animals. Place these books on shelves and into a basket. Place the basket near a new soft area, which is created by pillow stuffed into yellow and brown pillowcases. Add small stuffed wild animals for hugging while enjoying the books.

❒ Make available 10" x 11" newsprint, pointed markers, crayons, and pencils for the children to make books about "Wild Animals." The children can make their own pictures and then dictate what they want on each page. You can write their dictations onto each page or write individual words onto cards for the children to copy. The children work on their books over the entire theme period. When they are finished, they make a cover from construction paper. Each child's book is unique.

MANIPULATIVES EXPERIENCES

☐ Place a large set of Legos with zoo animals in a low-traffic area of the floor. Place the tub of Legos on a plywood geometric shape (see page 26) to help the children know where to keep their play.

☐ Place a large floor puzzle of a tiger in a low-traffic area of the room where up to four children can comfortably work.

MATH EXPERIENCE

☐ Place a tub of plastic zoo animals onto the floor next to a vinyl-graphing mat for the children to use to classify the animals. Also provide two clipboards with pencils for counting sets and writing numerals.

Bibliography

Bergen, D. (ed.) 1987. *Play as a medium for learning and development.* Portsmouth, NH: Heinemann.

Berk, L. E. 1994. Vygotsky's theory: The importance of make-believe play. *Young Children,* 50 (1), 30–39.

Berk, L. E. 1997. *Child development,* 4th ed. Boston: Allyn and Bacon.

Berk, L. E., and A. Winsler. 1995. *Scaffolding children's learning—Vygotsky and early childhood education.* NAEYC Research into Practice Series 7. Washington, DC: NAEYC.

Biber, B., E. Shapiro, and D. Wickens. 1971. *Promoting cognitive growth: A developmental interactional point of view.* Washington, DC: NAEYC.

Bodrova, E., and D. Leong. 2004. Observing play: What we see when we look at it through "Vygotsky's eyes." *Play, Policy and Practice Connections* 8 (1–2).

Bowman, K. 2009. The stick: An open-ended play classic. *Resources for imaginative play,* November 19. Retrieved from http://www.imaginativeplay.blogspot.com/2009_11_01_archive.html.

Bredekamp, S. (ed.). 1991. *Developmentally appropriate practice in early childhood programs serving children from birth through age eight.* Washington, DC: NAEYC.

Brown, M. H. 2000. Playing: The peace of childhood. *Young Children,* 55 (6), 36-37.

Brown, S., and C. Vaughan. 2009. *Play: How it shapes the brain, opens the imagination, and invigorates the soul.* New York: Penguin.

Bruner, J. S., A. Jolly, and K. Sylva. 1976. *Play: Its role in development and evolution.* New York: Basic Books.

Bultman, S. 1997. *The Froebel gifts 2000: The building gifts 2–6.* Grand Rapids: Uncle Goose Toys, Inc.

Burroughs, S., and R. Evans (eds.). 1986. *Play, language and socialization—Perspectives on adult roles.* New York: Gordon and Breach.

Burton, V. 1997. The developing brain. *Tampa Bay Baby,* 4–7.

Carlisle, A. 2001. Using the multiple intelligences theory to assess early childhood curricula. *Young Children*, 56 (6), 77–83.

Cartwright, S. 1988. Play can be the building blocks of learning. *Young Children,* 43 (5), 44–47.

Cartwright, S. 1990. Learning with large blocks. *Young Children,* 45 (3), 38–41.

Casey, B. M., N. Andrews, H. Schindler, J. E. Kersh, A. Samper, and J. Copley. 2008. The development of spatial skills through interventions involving block-building activities. *Cognition and Instruction,* 26 (3), 269–309.

Chalufour, I., and K. Worth. 2004. *Building structures with young children.* St. Paul, MN: Redleaf Press.

Cherry, C. 1979. *Creative play for the developing child.* Belmont, CA: David S. Lake.

Christie, J., and K. Roskos. 2006. Standards, science, and the role of play in early literacy education, in D. Singer, R. Golinkoff, and K. Hirsh-Pasek (eds.), *Play = learning: How play motivates and enhances children's cognitive and social-emotional growth.* Oxford, UK: Oxford University Press.

Christie, J. F., and F. Wardle. 1992. How much time is needed for play? *Young Children,* 47 (3), 28–31.

Cohen, L. 2006. *Young children's discourse strategies during pretend block play: A sociocultural approach.* PhD diss., New York: Fordham University.

Conrad, A. 1995. *Content analysis of block play literature.*(Report No. PS 023216). East Lansing, MI: National Center for Research on Teacher Learning. (ERIC Document Reproduction Service No. ED382357.)

Copley, J. V. 2000. *The young child and mathematics.* Washington, DC: NAEYC.

Corbett, B. 1988. *A garden of children.* Mississauga, ON: The Froebel Foundation.

Daniels, H. 2005. *An introduction to Vygotsky.* New York: Routledge.

Darling, J. 1994. *Child-centred education and its critics,* London: Paul Chapman.

DeVries, R., and L. Kohlberg. 1987. *Programs of early education: The constructivist view.* New York: Longman.

Drew, W. F. 2006. *Block play and performance standards: Using unstructured materials to teach academic content.* Presentation, NAEYC Conference, November 8.

Drew, W. F., J. Christie, J. E. Johnson, A. M. Meckley, and M. L. Nell. 2008. Constructive play: A value-added strategy for meeting early learning standards. *Young Children,* 63 (4), 38–44.

Drew, W. F., and B. Rankin. 2004. Promoting creativity for life using open-ended materials. *Young Children,* 59 (4), 38–45.

Easterly, G. 2002. Examining relationships between constructive play and language in preschool children. Unpublished diss., Tallahassee, FL: The Florida State University.

Elkind, D. E. 1988. *Miseducation: Preschoolers at risk.* New York: Alfred A. Knopf.

Elkind, D. E. 2007. *The power of play: Learning what comes naturally.* Philadelphia: Da Capo Press.

Erikson, E. H. 1963. *Childhood and society,* 2nd ed. New York: Norton.

Erikson, E. H. 1977. *Toys and reason.* New York: Norton.

Florida Department of Education, Office of Early Learning. 2005. *Florida Voluntary Prekindergarten Education Standards.* Tallahassee, FL: Florida Department of Education.

Florida Institute of Education. 2001. *Florida School Readiness Performance Standards for Three-, Four-, and Five-Year-Old Children 2002.* Tallahassee, FL: Florida Partnership for School Readiness.

Flynn, L. L., and J. Kieff. 2002. Including *everyone* in outdoor play. *Young Children,* 57 (3), 20–26.

Forman, G. E., and D. S. Kuschner. 1983. *Piaget for teaching children—The child's construction of knowledge.* Washington, DC: NAEYC.

Freud, A. 1968. *Normality and pathology in childhood: Assessments of development.* New York: International Universities Press.

Freud, A. 1971. *The ego and mechanisms of defense.* New York: International Universities Press.

Frost, J., and B. Klein. 1979. *Children's play and playgrounds.* Boston: Allyn and Bacon.

Galinsky, E. 2010. *Mind in the making: The seven essential life skills every child needs.* Washington, DC: NAEYC.

Gallacher, L. 2006. Block play, the sand pit and the doll corner: The (dis)ordering materialities of educating young children. Online papers series, Institute of Geography School of Geosciences, University of Edinburgh. www.era.lib.ed.ac.uk/handle/1842/1002

Gardner, H. 1983. *Frames of mind.* New York: Basic Books.

Gardner, H. 1993. *Multiple intelligences: The theory in practice.* New York: Basic Books.

Gardner, H. 1996. Are there additional intelligences? The case for naturalist, spiritual, and existential intelligences, in J. Kane (ed.). *Education, information and transformation.* Englewood Cliffs, NJ: Prentice Hall.

Garvey, C. 1977. *Play.* Cambridge, MA: Harvard University Press.

Geist, E. 2001. Children are born mathematicians: Promoting the construction of early mathematical concepts in children under five. *Young Children,* 56 (4), 12–19.

Gregory, K. M., A. S. Kim, and A. Whiren. 2003. The effect of verbal scaffolding on the complexity of preschool children's block constructions, in D. E. Lytle (ed.). *Play and educational theory and practice.* Westport, CT: Praeger Publishers.

Guanella, F. M. 1934. *Block building activities of young children.* New York: Archives of Psychology.

Guha, S. 2002. Integrating mathematics for young children through play. *Young Children,* 57 (3), 90–91.

Gura, P. 1992. *Exploring learning: Young children and block play.* London: The Froebel Blockplay Research Group.

Hanline, M. F., S. Milton, and P. Phelps. 2001. Young children's block construction activities: Findings from 3 years of observation. *Journal of Early Intervention,* 24 (3), 224–237.

Hanline, M. F., S. Milton, and P. Phelps. 2009. The relationship between preschool block play and reading and math abilities in early elementary school: A longitudinal study of children with and without disabilities. *Early Child Development and Care,* 180 (8), 1005–1017.

Hanna, S., and A. Wilford. 1990. *Floor time—Tuning in to each child.* New York: Scholastic.

Harms, T., D. Cryer, and R. M. Clifford. 1990. *Infant/toddler environment rating scale.* New York: Teachers College Press.

Harris, T. T., and J. D. Fuqua. 2000. What goes around comes around: Building a community of learners through circle times. *Young Children,* 55 (1), 44–47.

Hart, B., and T. R. Risley. 1995. *Meaningful differences in the everyday experience of young American children.* Baltimore, MD: Paul H. Brookes.

Helm-Harris, J., and L. Katz. 2011. *Young investigators: The project approach in the early years.* Washington, DC: NAEYC.

Hewitt, K. 2001. Blocks as a tool for learning: Historical and contemporary perspectives. *Young Children,* 56 (1), 6–13.

Hirsch, E. S. 1984. *The block book.* Washington, DC: NAEYC.

Hirsch, E. S. 1996. Block building: Practical considerations for the classroom teacher, in E. Hirsch (ed.). *The block book,* 3rd ed. Washington, DC: NAEYC.

Hirsh-Pasek, K., R. M. Golinkoff, and D. Eyer. 2003. *Einstein never used flash cards: How our children really learn and why they need to play more and memorize less.* Emmaus, PA: Rodale.

Hill-Clarke, K., and S. Colley. 2002. Promoting early literacy in the natural environment. *Dimensions of Early Childhood,* 30 (4), 10–16.

Hohmann, M., and D. P. Weikart. 1995. *Educating young children—Active learning practices for preschool and child care programs.* Ypsilanti, MI: HighScope Press.

Johnson, H. 1933. The art of block building, in E. Hirsch (ed.). 1996. *The block book,* 3rd ed. Washington, DC: NAEYC.

Johnson, J., J. Christie, and F. Wardle. 2005. *Play, development, and early education*. New York: Allyn and Bacon.

Johnson, L. V. 1957. A study of socialization in block play. *The Journal of Educational Research,* 50 (8), 623–626.

Jones, E., and G. Reynolds. 1992. *The play's the thing . . .Teachers' roles in children's play.* New York: Teachers College Press.

Kamii, C., and R. DeVries. 1978. *Physical knowledge in preschool education.* New Jersey: Prentice Hall.

Kostelnik, M. J., A. K. Soderman, and A. P. Whiren. 2007. *Developmentally Appropriate Curriculum: Best practice in early childhood education.* Upper Saddle River, NJ: Pearson/Merrill Prentice Hall.

Kramer, R. 1976. *Maria Montessori.* New York: G. P. Putman's Sons.

Krentz, A. A. 1998. *Play and education in Plato's* Republic. Paideia Project On-line, Twentieth World Congress of Philosophy, August 10–16. www.bu.edu/wcp/Papers/Educ/EducKren.htm

Kritchevsky, S., E. Prescott, and L. Walling. 1969. *Planning environments for young children: Physical space.* Washington, DC: NAEYC.

Lytle, D. E. (ed.). 2003. *Play and educational theory and practice.* Westport, CT: Praeger.

MacDonald, S. 2001. *Block play: The complete guide to learning and playing with blocks.* Silver Spring, MD: Gryphon House.

McCracken, J. B. 1987. *Play is FUNdamental.* Washington, DC: NAEYC.

McCracken, J. B. 2002. Theme issue on early literacy. *Dimensions of Early Childhood,* 30 (2), 1–32

McCune, L. 1995. A normative study of representational play at the transition to language. *Developmental Psychology,* 31 (2), 198–206.

McCune-Nicolich, L. 1981. Toward symbolic functioning: Structure of early pretend games and potential parallels with language. *Child Development,* 52, 785–797.

Miyakawa, Y., C. Kamii, and M. Nagahiro. 2005. The development of logico-mathematical thinking at ages 1–3 in play with blocks and an incline. *Journal of Research in Child Development,* 19, 292–301.

Montessori, M. 1964. *The Montessori method.* New York: Schocken.

Murray, A. 2001. Ideas on manipulative math for young children. *Young Children,* 56 (4), 28–29.

National Association for the Education of Young Children. 1966. *Montessori in Perspective.* Washington, DC: NAEYC

National Association for the Education of Young Children and the National Council for Teachers of Mathematics. 2010. *Early childhood mathematics: Promoting good beginnings.* Position statement. Washington, DC: NAEYC.

National Association for the Education of Young Children and the National Council of Teachers of Mathematics. 2002. Math experiences that count! *Young Children,* 57 (4), 60–62.

The National Research Council (ed.). 2000. *How people learn: Brain, mind, experience, and school.* Washington, DC: National Academy Press.

O'Brien, K. 1998. *Montessori and Catholicism.* Accessed September 21, 2001, at http://transporter.com/mcc.Essay02.htm (web page discontinued).

Olfman, S. (ed.). 2003. *All work and no play . . . How educational reforms are harming our preschoolers.* Westport, CT: Praeger Publishers.

Parten, M. B. 1932. Social participation among preschool children. *Journal of Abnormal Psychology,* 27, 243–269.

Phelps, P. C. 1986. An investigation of the functional relationship between play space allotments, play materials and the social behavior of toddlers. Unpublished diss. Tallahassee, FL: The Florida State University.

Phelps, P. C. 2007. *Beyond Centers and Circle Time Curriculum Pre-Kindergarten Theme Series.* Lewisville, NC: Kaplan Early Learning Company.

Phelps, P. C., and M. F. Hanline. 1999. Let's play blocks! Creating effective learning experiences for young children. *Teaching Exceptional Children,* 32 (2), 62–67.

Piaget, J. 1962. *Play, dreams and imitation in childhood.* New York: W.W. Norton.

Pickett, L. 1998. Literacy learning during block play. *Journal of Research in Childhood Education.* 12: 225–30.

Pratt, C. 1948. *I learn from children.* New York: Simon and Shuster.

Provenzo, E. F., and A. Brett. 1983. *The complete block book.* Syracuse, NY: Syracuse University Press.

Powell, J. 1998. *The Mozart connection.* Presentation, NAEYC Conference, November.

Reifel, S. 1982. The structure and content of early representational play: The case of building blocks, in S. Hill and B. J. Barnes (eds.). *Young children and their families,* Lexington, MA: Heath.

Reifel, S. 1984. Block construction: Children's developmental landmarks in representation of space. *Young Children,* 39 (3), 61–67.

Reifel, S. 1984. Symbolic representation at two ages: Block buildings of a story. *Discourse Processes,* 7, 11–20.

Rogers, C. S., and J. K. Sawyers. 1988. *Play in the lives of children.* Washington, DC: NAEYC.

Rogers, D. L. 1985. Blocks . . . Important materials in EC programs. *Early Child Development and Care,* 20, 245–261.

Roskos, K. and O. M. Hanbali. 2000. *Creating connections, building constructions: Language, literacy, and play in early childhood.* International Reading Association, Inc. http://www.readingonline. org/articles/art_index.asp?HREF=/articles/roskos/index.html

Rubin, K. H., T. L. Maioni, and M. Hornung. 1976. Free play behaviors in middle- and lower-class preschoolers: Parten and Piaget revisited. *Child Development,* 47, 414–419.

Rushton, S. 2001. Applying brain research to create developmentally appropriate learning environments. *Young Children,* 56 (5), 76–82.

Schomburg, R. Using symbolic play abilities to assess academic readiness. *Play, Policy, & Practice Connections.* Washington, DC: NAEYC. (Text available at www.webshares.northseattle.edu/ fam180/topics/agestages/usingsymplay.htm)

Segal, M. 1998. *Your child at play: Three to five years,* 2nd ed. New York: Newmarket Press.

Shore, R. 1997. *Rethinking the brain.* New York: Families and Work Institute.

Silber, K. 1965. *Pestalozzi: The man and his work,* 2nd ed. London: Routledge and Kegan Paul.

Smilansky, S. 1968. *The effects of sociodramatic play on disadvantaged preschool children.* New York: Wiley.

Smilansky, S. 1990. Sociodramatic play: Its relevance to behavior and achievement in school, in E. Klugman and S. Smilansky (eds.). *Children's play and learning.* New York: Teacher's College.

Smilansky, S., and L. Shefatya. 1990. *Facilitating play: A medium for promoting cognitive, social-emotional, and academic development in young children.* Gaithersburg, MD: Psychological and Educational Publications.

Soana, D. 2000. More about woodworking with young children. *Young Children,* 55 (2), 38–39.

Stannard, L., C. H. Wolfgang, I. Jones, and P. Phelps. 2001. A longitudinal study of the predictive relations among construction play and mathematical achievement. *Early Child Development and Care,* 167, 115–125.

Stanton, J., and A. Weisberg. 1996. Suggested equipment for block building, in E. Hirsch (ed.). *The block book,* 3rd ed. Washington, DC: NAEYC.

Tsao, Y. L. 2008. Using guided play to enhance children's conversation, creativity, and competence in literacy. *Education,* 128 (3), 515–520.

Vergeront, J. 1987. *Places and spaces for preschool and primary (indoors).* Washington, DC: NAEYC.

Vinson, B. M. 2001. Fishing and Vygotsky's concept of effective education. *Young Children,* 56 (1), 88–89.

Vygotsky, L. S. 1967. Play and its role in the mental development of the child. *Soviet Psychology,* 5 (3), 6–18.

Vygotsky, L. S. 1978. *Mind in society: The development of higher psychological processes,* 14th ed. Cambridge, MA: Harvard University Press.

Vygotsky L. S. 1986. *Thought and language,* rev. ed. Cambridge, MA: MIT Press.

Weikart, D., L. Rogers, C. Adcock, and D. McClelland. 1970. *The cognitively oriented curriculum: A framework for preschool teachers.* Washington, DC: NAEYC.

Weikart, D. P., J. T. Bond, and J. T. McNeil. 1978. *The Ypsilanti Perry Preschool Project: Preschool years and longitudinal results through fourth grade.* Ypsilanti, MI: HighScope Press.

Weikart, D. P., and L. J. Schweinhart. 1992. HighScope Preschool Program outcomes, in J. McCord and R. E. Tremblay (eds.). *Preventing antisocial behavior: Interventions from birth to adolescence.* New York: The Guilford Press.

Wellhousen, K., and J. Kieff. 2001. *A constructivist approach to block play in early childhood.* New York: Delmar.

Williams, C. K., and C. Kamii. 1986. How do children learn by handling objects? *Young Children,* 42 (1), 23–26.

Williams, M. S., and S. Shellenberger. 1992. *An introduction to "How does your engine run?" The alert program for self-regulation.* Albuquerque, NM: Therapy Works, Inc.

Wolfgang, C. H. 1977. *Helping passive and aggressive preschoolers through play.* Columbus, OH: Charles E. Merrill.

Wolfgang, C. H. 2004. *Child guidance through play: Teaching positive social behaviors (Ages 2–7).* Boston, MA: Pearson.

Wolfgang, C. H., L. L. Stannard, and I. Jones. 2001. Block play performance among preschoolers as a predictor of later school achievements in mathematics. *Journal of Research in Childhood Education,* 15 (2), 173–180.

Wolfgang, C. H., and M. E. Wolfgang. 1992. *School for young children: Developmentally appropriate practices.* Boston: Allyn and Bacon.

Index